Ableton Live 5

TIPS AND TRICKS   Martin Delaney

PC Publishing

PC Publishing
Keeper's House
Merton
Thetford
Norfolk IP25 6QH
UK

Tel +44 (0)1953 889900
Fax +44 (0)1953 889901
email info@pc-publishing.com
website http://www.pc-publishing.com

First published 2006

© PC Publishing

ISBN 1 870775 090

British Library Cataloguing in Publication Data
A catalogue record for this book is available from the British Library

Cover design by Hilary Norman Design Ltd

Printed and bound in Great Britain by Biddles, Kings Lynn, Norfolk

Contents

A manual, a tip, a trick, what's the difference?

RTFM, people say on the internet, Read The F****** Manual; a rude way of making a good point. And now – it's my turn to say to you – as nicely as possible – RTFM!

Ableton Live 5 Tips and Tricks is NOT intended to be a rehash of the excellent Live 5 manual, which you already have on your computer in pdf form, accessible via Read the Live Manual in the Live Help menu (if you bought a boxed copy of Live, you have a printed copy too - and some cool stickers). Although there's inevitable crossover with the Live documentation, the things in this book have arisen through experimentation and experience (and, sometimes, asking other people). Amongst other things, this book's about how Live interacts with the user, and with the outside world, in the form of musicians, other computers, peripherals, and almost-essentials such as audio/MIDI interfaces and hardware controllers. As the old saying goes, 'No Live user is an island'.

Ableton Live isn't a regular DAW – Digital Audio Workstation (pronounced 'door' – horrible, isn't it?) – and anything written about it has to reflect that. It's common to play software instruments within Cubase or Logic, but, although Live also hosts software instruments in various forms, it can be considered an instrument in its own right.

Live 5 does everything you want it to – you just don't know it yet

Whenever it's possible, I work exclusively with Live – getting to know it better, and using workrounds to achieve results that would otherwise need other software/hardware. You might be surprised at what this simple-looking software can manage with a bit of deviousness.

Who is this book for?

The newcomer: if you're in the early Live-curious stages of use, this book will give you a kick-start with some of the concepts and applications that are possible with Live, saving you weeks of fiddling, probing, and head-scratching, so you can get to the sweet stuff ASAP. It's not the same as the manual.

For the intermediate user: This book will introduce you to Live features that you might not have encountered yet – maybe you've been too busy, or maybe you've got too comfortable in those cosy old ways, unaware of the thrills that this latest update brings. It's not the same as the manual.

For the advanced user: As well as showing you new features and nutty ideas, I've included reminders of more commonly-known Live features. Some of these reminders involve stating the obvious – I don't know about you, but sometimes I need that. There are so many things to learn, and working habits are so easy to get into, that you just can't retain it all. And if you don't even recognise the thing I'm 'reminding' you of – just keep it to yourself and nobody will ever know...you can do the same for me some time. There's a lot going on beneath the surface with Live, more than ever with Live 5 and it's sneaky new context menu. By the way, did I say it's not the same as...ah, now you're getting the idea!

For those using a cracked copy of Live: do everybody a favour and buy it. Those features you're enjoying didn't just fall out of the ideas tree straight into your computer; people have invested a lot of time and creativity to bring you Live. Before pleading poverty, consider that you may qualify for an educational discount, and remember that 'Lite' versions of Live are often included with audio hardware packages, from people like M-Audio, Mackie, and Tascam, giving you a convenient all-in-one affordable way into the Live-plus-hardware experience.

Learning curve of enlightenment – or twisted pretzel of confusion?

Because Live leads a dual existence as a performance instrument and studio tool, it can be tricky to organise a book like this one; it has to be categorised somehow. Where relevant, I've put common things together – items common to all arenas of Live use. I've also used (very broad) sections to cover more specific Live activities. There's a huge amount of crossover in everything that Live does, so don't be surprised if certain features pop up in unexpected places.

There are Info boxes dotted around, containing supplementary bits of information designed to enhance your reading experience. These boxes are generally connected to the content of the page you're reading, but more abstract comments will appear from time to time – there's one in the margin here.

The test rig

I'm a Mac user, but I've endeavoured to keep everything cross-platform in this book, and to accommodate users of all kinds of computers and hardware. However, it might be useful for you to know what my basic set-up was while writing this book:

• Apple G4 PowerBook 12inch, 1.5 GHz, 1.25 GB RAM, 80 GB hard drive.
• Lacie FireWire-bus powered hard drives.
• Edirol FA-66 FireWire audio/MIDI interface.
• Evolution UC33e USB MIDI controller.
• Griffin Technology PowerMate USB controller.

I hope you get something positive from reading this book; what I most want to do is encourage you to try new things with Live, to experiment...do something that you wouldn't usually do with it. Catch you later!

About the author

I'm Martin Delaney; pleased to meet you.

I've been using Ableton Live since version 1.0.1, back in 2001, and I'll probably be using it until version 58.1 or I drop, whichever comes first. Before Live came along I'd played exactly ONE live show; although I'd been creating music for years, I wasn't a 'musician' – I don't really sing or play any instruments – I was just into songwriting and sequencing and making an electronic noise, so there wasn't a comfortable way for me to present my music in a live environment. Eventually I bit the bullet, and hauled my 'studio' on stage for that one gig. Although it worked okay, it was a big hassle, and not quite what I wanted to do.

Shortly after this gig, my friend Paul Wiffen (writing in Sound On Sound) mentioned an intriguing new software product called Ableton Live. I emailed Paul with a couple of questions, then rushed to the Ableton website and bought Live. At the time I was jamming at home on an iBook with dozens of QuickTime Pro files looping on screen; it was fun, but there was no easy way to organise or record what happened. I initially saw Live as a way of organising that chaos by saving my QuickTime loops in the Session View's grid. It's come a long way since then, though that jamming ability is still what makes Live work for me – I now use Live in all musical situations: performing, composing, recording, jamming, and remixing. I also teach Live on a one-to-one basis to other musicians, and to groups of students, as part of my activity with Public Loop.

Last year my book Laptop Music was published by PC Publishing, who have brought you this title too; in Sound On Sound, Martin Walker (obviously a man of taste) wrote: "Overall, I loved this book's streetwise approach – it's one of the most entertaining music technology reads I've ever had, and well worth the money!"; us Martins have to stick together.

What's that you're asking? What do I do when I'm not working with Ableton Live? I, er...um...well, you keep in touch now

Ableton Live is my instrument.

Acknowledgments

Personal

Jan Anderson: without her help, nothing gets done; Carey Armstrong: just is – and always will be; Grace Connor: she must learn to use her powers for the good of humankind; Dad, my brothers, their families: life's too short, we don't spend enough time together; Piney Gir for the great gigs; mindlobster for immersive audio-visual onslaught; Paul Newman for the employment opportunities; the people I've worked with lately – Analog vs Digital, Funsize Lions, Glideascope, J-Lab, Last Precious Cookie, Motormark, Piney Gir, Vic Twenty, Vocoder, Wired Women; the exceptionally fine people at Truck Festival 2005; Darren and Yuki at the Hat On Wall; Andi and Alex at After-Dinner Recordings.

For the book

Phil Chapman at PC Publishing; Alexandra at Behringer for the FCB1010; Conny and John at Edirol for the FA-66; Mathias at Faderfox for the DJ-1, LV-1, and LX-1; Colin at M-Audio for the Trigger Finger. Jody Wisternoff; the Live lab rats: Glideascope, J-Lab, Saytek, Songcarver.

At Ableton

Dave Hill Jr, Anita Lotterschmidt, Jesse Terry, Christian Kleine, Gerhard Behles, Robert Henke, and all the other Abletons. Thanks for enabling us to make music the way we always wanted to…and for keeping it on track…and for the quality control!

And...

Every friendly and curious face I meet when I'm out there with my laptop, running Ableton Live on stage, in studios, or jamming and writing in coffee shops…

Images/quotes

All product photos courtesy of the relevant manufacturers.
Apple hardware images courtesy of Apple.
Hardware photos by Martin Delaney.
J-Lab photo by Martin Delaney.
Hans Zimmer quote from the Ableton website.
See the 'Links' section in the Appendix for website addresses.

What's new (and old) in Live 5?

It's tempting to skip the entire 'what is Ableton Live and what does it do?' routine – as you've gone to the trouble of picking up this book then you must already have some idea of what Live is about – you've bought it, or have at least downloaded the demo. If you don't yet have Live 5 in full or demo form, grab it from the Ableton site now. If you're a fully-functioning user of a previous version, that goes for you too – you'll be surprised at how Live has evolved. And while you're there, check for upgrade opportunities and bundle offers. And t-shirts. And bags.

But you know, maybe we should prod our memories; we can remind ourselves why we're here, and what our common interests are – the abiding concepts that made Live so exciting in the first place...

What is Ableton Live?

Ableton Live is the cross-platform software that changed the music world – not just the music software world. Live has gathered fans – in a way usually associated with performers rather than software – as it has matured into a

Live Session View

1

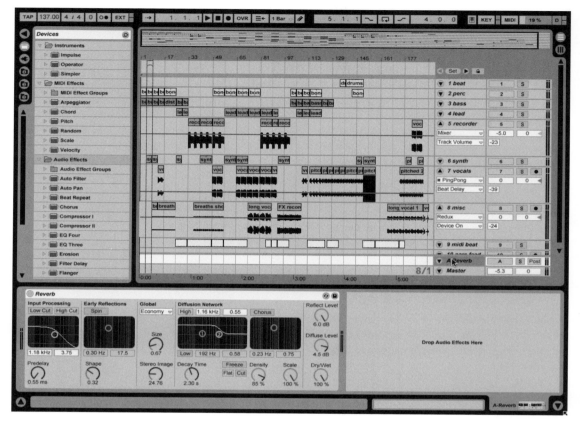

Live Arrangement View

credible alternative to established software workstations – the DAWs I mentioned in the introduction.

Live was created by Robert Henke and Gerhard Behles, beginning as a
simple loop-based jamming tool with a unique interface. At a time when
music software designers were continuing to produce interfaces that imitat-
ed hardware, Live looked like something derived from spreadsheet, web, and
game design – which doesn't sound very 'musical', but...it is. Not only did
Live allow a computer to become a sampling instrument capable of real-time
performance, it retained many functions of 'traditional' music sequencing/
recording, with it's two 'views' – Session and Arrangement. An instrument
that records itself, but which can also record other instruments – interesting
(also the cause of mucho confusion for newcomers). Another quirk – despite
its 'futuristic' nature, Live embraces some of the oldest principles of electronic music, especially those relating to sampling, with its focus on mangling
chunks of sound. Live's follow actions – 'random' playback elements with a
degree of user-definability – are reminiscent of generative music (especially
given the chaotic possibilities I'll discuss in Chapter 7 'Live Talks To Itself'),
Operator includes FM-style synthesis, and Live 5 includes an arpeggiator;
hardly innovative, but imbued with typical Ableton style.

Arpeggiator and Operator

So, here's a reminder of what Live does.

Session and Arrangement Views
The two faces of Live: the Session View, built for performance and jamming; and the Arrangement View, optimised for more considered song-building tasks. Whatever happens, you'll be working in both of these views, so get used to them.

Audio and MIDI clips
These are Live's core components: audio or MIDI segments that can be recorded, edited, triggered, looped, stretched, transposed, processed, auto-mated, and grouped (as scenes).

Warping
This is what Live's all about. The timing of an audio clip can be changed by the insertion of warp markers – a drum hit (or any part of any sound) can be moved to fall exactly on a beat or a division of a beat. You can change not only the tempo, but the rhythmic nature of any audio – altering the groove of a drum loop, or transforming a recording of a faulty air conditioning unit into a rhythm part. All without stopping the song!

Time stretching algorithms for a range of material
Audio clips can be assigned individual time stretching algorithms, for instance 'Beats' or 'Tones' – though you don't have to use the 'right' one, by any means; not only doesn't the 'right' one always work best, you'll get some interesting effects by using the 'wrong' one.

Native, Audio Unit, and VST instruments and effects
Live includes a suite of Devices – audio effects (Auto Filter for example), MIDI effects (like the Arpeggiator), and three instru-ments; Operator, Simpler, and Impulse. It's also compatible with third-party Audio Unit and VST plug-ins – the Live instru-ments and effects can't be used directly with other sequencers.

Auto filter

MIDI and computer keyboard mapping options for real-time triggering
Nearly all of Live's functions are assignable to MIDI and comput-er keyboard commands, emphasising real-time control and minimising mouse work. Not only can you trigger a particular loop or activate an effect via MIDI, you can select tracks, scroll through clips, start/stop playback, and much more.

Collage style of working
Sounds from different sources (and of different formats and sample rates) can be added and manipulated in real time. Freely combine parts from software instruments, with your audio recordings, and material from CDs, the internet.

MIDI recording

Work with MIDI in a linear 'sequencing' fashion in the Arrangement View, or jam with MIDI clips in the Session View. Import a MIDI file (the whole thing or selected tracks), draw in notes with the pencil tool, or record notes played on Live's 'pseudo' MIDI keyboard, or via an external MIDI keyboard controller.

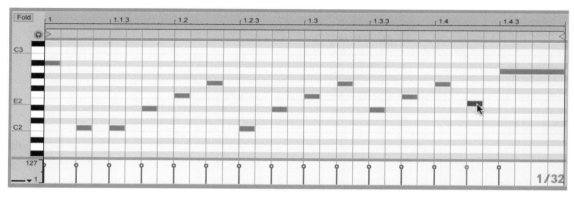

Drawing in MIDI notes

Multitrack audio recording

Record multiple audio tracks simultaneously – as many as your audio interface and your computer will tolerate, going through the entire recording process without hitting 'stop'; use MIDI to control record functions.

Routing options

Tap tempo

Tap tempo makes beat matching easier – useful for DJs, and Live players working alongside 'real' instruments.

Routing options

Live has the simplest routing system around – but that doesn't mean 'basic'. Audio and MIDI can be routed between tracks, and effects send/returns created, with just a few clicks. Create audio submixes and bounces, send MIDI info to different instruments simultaneously, share one processor-hungry effect (such as reverb) across several tracks.

ReWire compatibility

ReWire synchronises Live with other music software, such as Logic, Cubase, and Reason. Use it to exploit the best qualities of different applications. It also facilitates movie scoring, when used with the ReVision ReWire movie player.

Info – Session vs Arrangement

Some Live users don't grasp the relationship between the Arrangement and Session Views, working in one, and regarding the 'other' as a mysterious place that requires a passport and vaccinations to visit. Please explore and understand the relationship between Arrangement and Session; in time, working across them becomes second nature. It's easy enough to do – just hit the tab key!

Who is Live for? How do they use it?

Live's performance angle was the thing that initially attracted experimentalists and jammers, but since then it's been adopted by instrumentalists, DJs, remixers, producers and composers, working in all fields of music. They use Live because of the real-time manipulation, friendly interface and flexibility – it encourages you to find connections and workrounds that you didn't know existed.

Quote

'For me, the overall best thing about Live 5 is its ability to manipulate audio in ways that ProTools and Logic do not possess. Changing the feel and swing of a loop by adjusting its warp points produces results that were previously unrealistic. The compositional power of Live is now on a par with Logic and Pro Tools. All this, and I haven't even mentioned its live performance features, which are unique and in a class of their own.' – *Jody Wisternoff, Way Out West*

In Live, tasks like 'performer' and 'composer' bleed into each other – the composer is now a performer, and the performer creates songs in real-time, recording his jams for subsequent refinement.

- Composers – create new parts and rearrange songs without ever hitting 'stop'; skip between the Session and Arrangement Views for uninterrupted stream-of-consciousness creativity.
- Laptop jammers – go to the club and dismantle your carefully-crafted studio work, or go on stage with an empty Session View, and build a soundscape as you go; record it all and burn it to CD or post it online the same night.
- Band members – put Live at the heart of your on-stage technology – to use a very abused phrase, it's your digital music hub!
- Soloists, vocalists and instrumentalists – run backing tracks, host software instruments, and process your sound in real time. Control Live from a MIDI keyboard, a MIDI pickup on your instrument, or from a MIDI pedal.
- Sound designers – create evolving sound textures in real-time. Use it in the theatre to deliver sound effects and cues right on time, in a flexible way that accommodates the vagaries of live performance.
- Soundtrack composers – stretch your music and other audio to fit that last-minute edit. Sync Live to Logic, DIgital Performer, Cubase, or ReVision for accurate cuts.
- Producers – record multitrack audio, then manipulate it – fast – in ways that leave other DAWs in the dust.
- Remixers – use Live to create alternative mixes, tempos, sounds, effects, and beats. Make original tracks fit entirely different beats and tempos.
- DJs – use Live's auto-warping to have a stack of MP3s in your songs folder, ready to drop into your set at any time. Throw in more beats, sounds, and effects. Use Live's crossfader and Re-Pitch warp mode for old-school DJ action.

Live's Info View

Support is available online

Info – you need help

Hit '?' to access Live's Info View, at the bottom left of your screen, for info about the interface object you're mousing over. If that isn't enough info, next stop should be the Help menu, where you can access the lessons, Live manual, or follow a link to the website.

What's new in Live 5?

Live 5 introduces major features and minor tweaks, supplying the features most-requested by Live users, while remaining true to the original Live concepts:

More DJ/remix-friendly features

The aforementioned Auto-Warp, Complex Warp Mode, expanded crossfader mapping, and support for more file formats (see below), all add to the DJ-friendliness of Live.

Locators

Locators are now featured in the Arrangement view

Locators (markers) are now featured in the Arrangement view; useful for jumping around your song. They are keyboard and MIDI-mappable, and quantized; try jamming in the Arrangement view by jumping between locators!

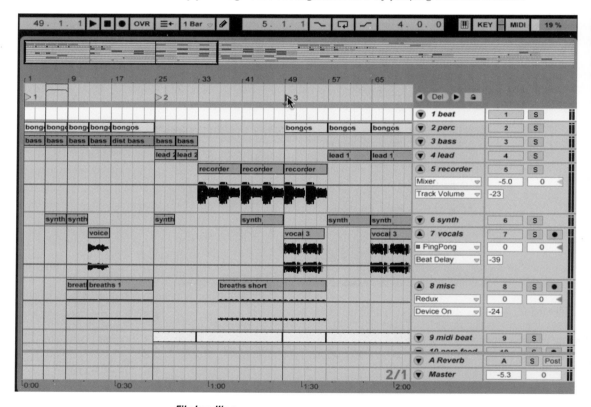

File handling

Live now imports MP3, Ogg Vorbis, Ogg FLAC and FLAC audio files. None of these compressed formats sound as good as full-quality WAVs or AIFs, but they are useful if you're grabbing sounds off the internet. Live 5 doesn't export in any of these file formats!

Organisation

It may not look much different, but the browser has been overhauled, with a search function amongst other additions. The Live Clip format has been introduced, and Live sets (or their individual elements) can be dragged directly into an open set.

Library

Live has a library now. This can be supplemented with (of course) your own material, or Live Packs, available from Ableton. See 'Get Organised' for more on Live Clips, the library, and associated developments.

Arrangement

As well as the locators mentioned above, the Arrangement View now features scrubbing. Click anywhere in the scrub area (above the tracks) to play from that point – it's quantized, like the locators. Also, the In/Out menu is now fully accessible from the Arrangement View.

Clip handling

Nudge buttons have been added to the Clip box, making it possible to 'bump' the start point of a playing clip backward or forward. Multiple clips can be selected, enabling certain parameters to be altered as a group – such as quantization, groove, transposition – and colour!

Live's library

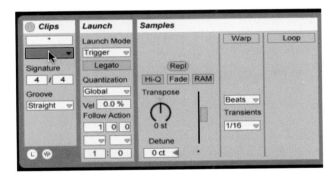

These are the parameters available with multiple clips selected

Track handling

Track Freeze gives your CPU a break by temporarily 'rendering' all clips in a track (audio or MIDI). Track Delay allows the start time of each individual track to be adjusted in milliseconds – it can't be used when device delay compensation is inactive.

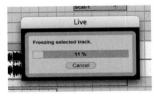

Track freeze in progress

MIDI editing

MIDI quantization options have been enhanced, and the Preview button in the MIDI Editor allows notes to be heard as they're drawn in or repositioned.

MIDI and computer keyboard remote control

The popular Mackie Control hardware controller is supported, and computer keyboard mapping has been expanded to include most of the keyboard – not just letters, but numbers and symbols too. The crossfader's MIDI mapping has also received an overhaul.

Live's Context menu

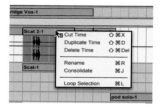

Count in

Devices

Live 5 features new audio and MIDI effects, such as the long-awaited Arpeggiator, a Flanger, and a Phaser, and updates to Simpler and Operator. Device presets are now accessed via the Browser, and combinations of effect devices can be saved as Device groups.

Miscellaneous stuff

Context menus are now available for many of Live's controls. There is now (finally) a count-in available for recording! Set it up in Preferences/Misc/ Behavior.

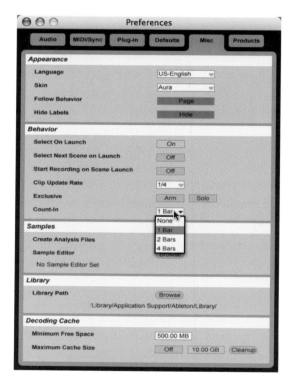

Info – one for the to-do list

Live doesn't export all tracks as separate files with a single command, like Logic's 'Export/all tracks as audio files'. This would be useful when sending tracks to users of other DAWs.

Get organised

Don't panic – I'll keep the 'sensible' stuff to a minimum; you've probably got a computer and installed Live already, so let's skim through that quickly and get on to some need-to-know stuff – the necessities of Live Life, the things that have to be done before you can start rockin; a little learning, a little housekeeping, some practical stuff, some organisation – how to collate the many samples and presets that you've generated, and Ten Top Transitional Tips for people coming to Live 5 from other sequencers such as Cubase, GarageBand, Logic – and Live 4.

First things – very first things...

Installation

Downloading, purchasing, and registering Live is all covered perfectly well in the Ableton manual, and on their website; it's really quite simple, and I have no interesting anecdotes to add on these subjects...sorry.

Mac or PC?

To answer a question with a question – does it matter? In many ways, Macs and PCs are running pretty equal these days. Macs have fallen behind in processor statistics, but it takes more than the biggest GHz to make the best computer platform – I believe that ease of use and reliability are more important, and in these respects OSX remains far superior to Windows XP.

System requirements

These are the recommended system requirements for Live 5: Mac: G3 or faster, 512 MB RAM, OSX 10.2.8 or later. Windows: 600 MHz CPU or faster, 512 MB RAM, Windows 2000/XP, compatible soundcard. For any music purposes, the faster your computer, the more RAM you have, and the bigger your drive, the better! If you haven't maxed out your RAM yet, please do so as soon as possible.

Check for updates

Take frequent trips to the Ableton website to ensure you have the very latest version. Ableton are refreshingly honest about posting bug fixes, and their updates are always worth having.

Lessons Table of Contents

Read the Live Manual...

Visit ableton.com...
Join the User Forum...
Get Support...

Check for Updates...

Live's Check for Updates menu item

9

Cracks

Yes, there are illegally 'cracked' copies of Live floating around the internet – see my earlier comments about this. If nothing else, be warned that they don't work very well, and those who use cracked copies of Live eventually admit defeat and pay for the real thing.

Another use for Demo Mode

If you're taking Live onstage, burn a CD containing the Live installer and your final Live set. If your computer develops any problems, install Live on another computer, and run it in Demo Mode for the gig (it's probably best not to have any third-party effects or instruments in your set, unless you can easily install them on a 'strange' computer too).

Managing your computer's resources

The things that most affect your computer's ability to deal with Live are decided when you buy it. Factors like clock speed (in MHz or GHz) and system bus bandwidth (how much data can flow through at one time), and drive speed (in RPM) all affect performance. The general computer 'tips' apply – it's just stating the obvious, like shut down any unnecessary applications or processes; the less your computer has to do at one time, the happier it'll be; more screen space is useful; more money will buy you more tracks and more simultaneously effects.

There are many ways to reduce CPU usage in Live. Turn off anything in Live that isn't necessary, especially effects that aren't in use. Disable any unused mono or stereo audio inputs, and put effects on return tracks. If you're working with instruments such as Impulse or Operator, turn off any unused LFOs or filters, and reduce the number of voices available – this goes for third-party instruments too. Avoid using the Reverb's 'First Class' Global setting. Be discriminating with the Hi-Q clip option, use mono samples wherever possible, and trim off unwanted parts of audio clips. You'll be amazed at how small a complete Live set can be. If you render any MIDI instrument clips, and unusual effects, to audio clips, your set will also run more easily during performances – and don't forget the new track freeze option (see 'Performance Notes').

What hardware do you need?

At the lowest level, you need headphones and audio cables to run Live – nothing else, it's all USB candy and FireWire treats. That's the Zen way. In reality, the world is full of fun stuff to give you more 'hands-on' control, and better quality audio in/out (with more channels). Work with Live on its own for a while, before spending money on extras – your ideas about 'ideal' accessories will change quickly.

Signal routing and I/O

When it comes to routing audio and MIDI, Live gives you the best of all possible worlds; the concepts are simple to understand, but the potential is there to create powerful set-ups. Audio from a particular track can go to the send/return channels, the master output, the cue output for pre listening,

---

Info

A very common error with my students – if you suddenly lose your Live audio out, make sure that you haven't got any effects like Gate, EQ3, or Auto Filter, on extreme settings that will totally silence a track (or the entire set if they're on the master track)...also look out for any Arrangement View automation that you may have forgotten about, such as fade outs...oops!

and to any other audio track in your Live set, including multiple tracks simultaneously. It's the same story with MIDI – send MIDI to several tracks with different audio instruments simultaneously, combine several MIDI tracks into one, send/receive MIDI to/from external software and hardware. A good starting point is to set your inputs to either 'no input' or 'external in', and your outputs to 'master', and then change them as necessary. I/O is another suspect if you're getting Live Set Silence – keep an eye on your ins and outs!

The Cue Out menu

Do the Lessons

Live includes great Lessons, available via View/Lessons. Study them all, even if at first glance they don't seem relevant to you; the Operator tutorials are particularly useful if you're having trouble figuring out what that interface is about!

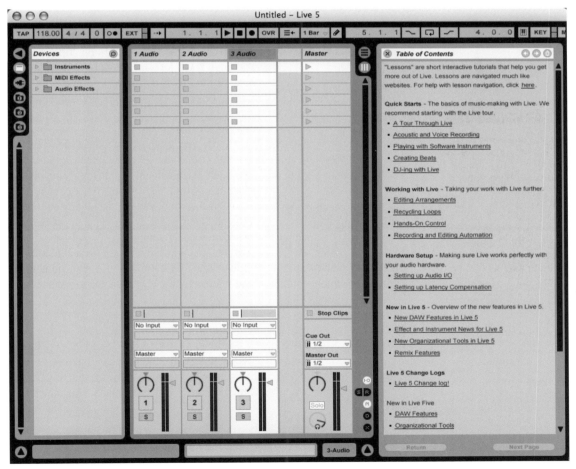

Live lessons

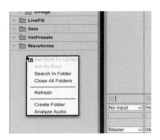

The context menu for library

Shortcuts

Live has always been great for keyboard shortcuts – see the full list in the Live manual; you'll have favourite shortcuts already, but there are probably others you'd use, if only you remembered them. Live 5 expands on this by adding context menus, which include items only available via shortcuts. You can try the context menu on any part of Live's interface – right-click (PC) or ctrl-click (Mac) – and see what pops up; for example the context menu will show quite different things in the Browser (search in folder, create folder, analyze audio, are a few) or in the MIDI Editor (Adaptive Grid, Fixed Grid, Draw Mode). See my top ten keyboard shortcuts at the back of this book.

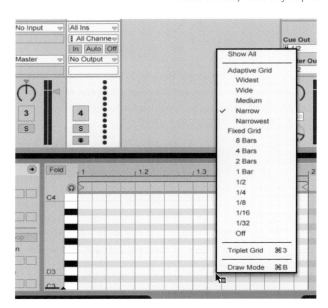

(Above) Context menu for MIDI clip editor

(Right) Audio output preferences

Configuring – sending audio/MIDI to audio/MIDI hardware

In Preferences you can determine which Input and Output Audio Devices Live uses (only one of each – with a few exceptions), buffer size and latency, and sample rate. Once you've selected the relevant hardware, use the Channel Configuration buttons to choose exactly which inputs/outputs Live will use – you can set these to mono or stereo, and remember to save CPU by disabling any that you won't be using. These configurations aren't set in stone – they'll change whenever you add new hardware, or if you work without your regular set-up, using your computer's standard soundcard instead.

Info

If the In/Out section doesn't show the options that you think should be available, go to Preferences, and check that Live's identified your audio/MIDI hardware. Even if the hardware is listed, you still need to activate the relevant ins/outs in the list, before they're available.

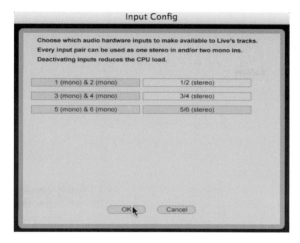

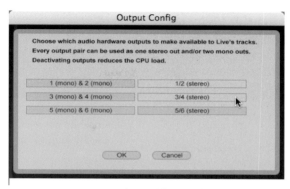

Input and Output config panels

Managing files and sets

The File Browser enhancements are the most exciting new features in Live 5. Why is this 'admin' stuff sexy? Because it'll save you heaps of time, and help you organise your source material in a logical and accessible way. It's now possible to drop entire Live sets, or their elements, from the Browser, directly into a new Live set. On the same theme, the File menu now includes a long overdue 'open recent Live set' item, and audio files can be dragged into Live's Session or Arrangement Views directly from your desktop; they can't be dragged out the same way though!

Info

Self contained sets are important, for backing up your files or sharing projects with other people – they save copies of all relevant audio files in a new folder. You know this already!

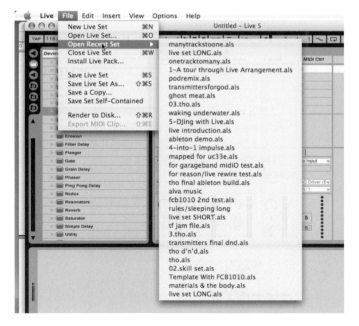

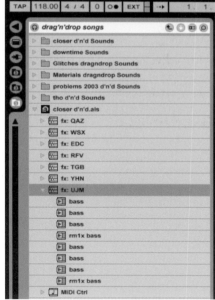

Open recent set menu item (left) and
Browsing/loading of sets (right)

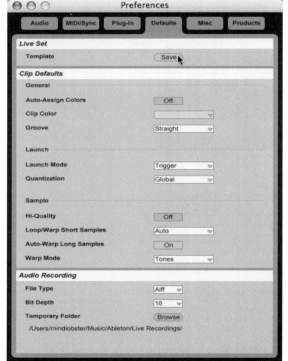

Info

You can render audio or MIDI clips to disk directly from the Session View. Remember to specify the length in bars and to stop or mute all unwanted clips!

Keeping file sizes down

In the interests of disk space, RAM, and CPU preservation, it will behove you (yes, behove) to keep your audio files small. There are various ways to do this:

- Record audio in mono when possible (use Channel Configuration/Input Config to enable this).
- Convert stereo clips to mono if stereo isn't required – do this by resampling (recording to another track), or rendering to disk (remembering to choose Convert to Mono) and reimporting.
- Reduce the sample rates and bit rates of audio files. Live can play clips of different sample rates together quite happily.
- Saving Live sets as self-contained (see above) helps with this too. When you close a self-contained Live set, it prompts you to discard any now-unused audio files.
- Once you've decided which portion of a particular clip you want to use, use an audio editor to trim the ends off. No audio editor? Well, there is another way...read about consolidation in the 'Clips And Scenes...' chapter.
- Clip RAM Mode, activated by the RAM switch in the Clip View, is used to load the currently selected audio clip into your computer's RAM; this can help take the load off your hard drive if it's struggling to read enough tracks at once. However, this obviously increases RAM usage – a trade-off.

Templates

In 'Preferences/Defaults/Live Set/Template' there's a little 'Save' button. Click on this and your current Live set will be saved as a template; all new Live sets you create will be based on this model – great if you have a favourite setup that you use for all your songs. A template includes all tracks, routings, MIDI and computer keyboard mappings, devices, and clips – although it won't act as a self-contained document, so if you move the audio flies referred to by your template's clips, then – too bad. It's been suggested that Live might one

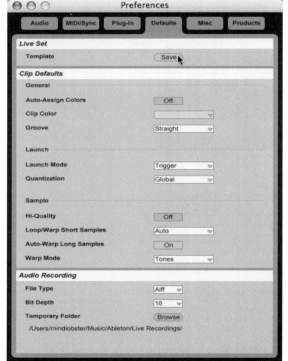

Save template button

Overwrite template alert

day save multiple templates, Logic-style, but the recent changes to the Browser and the introduction of the Library probably make this redundant.

The Browser

The Browser has become the centre of the Live universe, and it's going to be your best friend when it comes to organisational matters. Use it to browse and load device presets, to search, browse, preview, and load audio files, and to create, rename, or delete folders. MIDI files appear as folders containing individual tracks, ready to drag into your set. Double-click a folder to make it the root for a File Browser slot. You'll find that you're always changing your default Browser folders; at the moment mine are

1   Library
2   Current Live sets
3   Unarchived samples

iTunes is a great 'accessory' for the Live Browser – see 'Get More Sounds'.

Browsing device presets

itunes in the Browser

Just as MIDI files can now be cracked open in the Browser, so can Live sets. They function like folders – open a Live set 'folder' and you'll see sub-folders relating to each track, and within each track sub-folder you'll see all the clips contained within that track. These can be previewed and dragged into your current set just like any other Live Clip. The big news though, is that you can also drag the entire set into your current one; if there aren't enough tracks in the current set, new ones will be created. This enables you to easi-ly build a new Live set using sections from previous ones – about time!

- You could go on stage with just your first song loaded, then decide the running order of your set on the fly (every technical book has to say 'on the fly', it's in the rules).
- This method could also help if you don't have enough memory to load enormous Live sets – you can just load a few songs at a time.
- Dropping in new sets is smooth – you can do it while the previous song is playing, and there won't be any dropouts.
- If you can come up with a standard format for your Live set – the same number of tracks every time, for example – then you can drop in new songs without worrying about creating extra tracks, or loading extra effects.

Info – create a standard format for Live sets

When I'm putting a new tune together, it can go lots of different ways; it's not possible to have a consistent template for that situation - varying numbers of software instruments, audio clips, MIDI envelopes, ReWiring to Logic or Reason. When I'm preparing my Live performance sets, though, I do stick to a formula. All software instruments and automation are rendered to audio clips. I mix down from the original number of tracks to 6 (currently - that's always subject to review), and choose a 'generic' set of send effects that'll work in a performance situation. Finally, I map MIDI or computer keyboard remote control (or both) - depending on what hardware I aim to use for that night. By keeping the same layout every time, it's possible to have a library of 'drag'n'drop songs, ready to throw into my performance at any time.

The Library

Click the 'Library' button at top right of the File Browser to jump to the Library. By default you'll see folders for Clips, Sets, and Waveforms. If you use any Tacklebox products (covered in 'Get More Sounds'), you'll also see a LiveFill folder. The Clips folder contains a number of Live Clips (see below), the Sets folder is now the default location for Live Sets, and the Waveforms folder contains a selection of waveforms suitable for use in Live's sampling devices. The default Live 5 Library content is built from Live Packs, also covered in 'Get More Sounds'. Technically speaking, all Live device presets are now part of the Library too, which is why they're accessed via the Browser window. Use the context menu to delete items from the Library.

Moving to Live 5? Ten top transitional tips

Live 5 isn't like other sequencers; sometimes Live 5 isn't even like earlier versions of Live. If you're a long-term user of another sequencer, there'll be a period of adjustment...

1 Be patient. In my teaching experience, newbies have an advantage, they don't have preconceptions about where things are supposed to be or how they should work.
2 if you're used to working with beats in a certain way, or time stretching in a certain way. forget it. Live is flexible and real-time; nothing matches it for spontaneous manipulation of audio.
3 Understand the relationship between the Session and Arrangement Views; this is critical to getting the most out of Live.
4 There are some things that Live won't do, and that's where ReWire comes in handy, so you can get the best out of your 'old-world' sequencer and Live.
5 Look at Live with wide open eyes – the routing, the devices, the preferences; the solutions to many problems are right there.
6 The multi-clip assignments are real time-savers.
7 Work that browser hard – with a search function, the ability to rename items, and dragndrop creation of a library of sounds. All device preset browsing happens here now.
8 Your homework is to do the Live 5 Lessons – this is time well spent; the best possible introduction to the Live world view.
9 Remind yourself that Live can now open AIFs, WAVs, FLAC, Ogg FLAC, Ogg Vorbis, and MP3 files.
10 Live 5 adds mapping for many extra computer keys – exactly how many depends on your keyboard, I guess!! Now all numerical keys, and symbols such as / or [can be used – and their upper case counterparts too.

Clips and scenes, and a little on tracks

Clips and scenes are what the Session View grid is made of: clips are stacked vertically in tracks, and organised horizontally in scenes. Clips come in audio and MIDI varieties, while scenes are just – scenes. Let's start by looking at what clips have in common, rather than the differences...

Clips in general

Clips are the building blocks of Live. Any segment of audio or MIDI that you use in Live is a clip (there's also the new Live Clip format – see 'Get Organised'); a clip can even contain automation or MIDI bank/program info, without any notes at all. Whatever type of clip you're talking about, they have common features and behaviours, and Live 5 has added some new wrinkles.

I'll assume you're mostly familiar with what clips are, and how they work; that leaves us free to look at the more interesting clip qualities, beginning with the shared attributes of audio and MIDI clips.

Live 5 has new features which are common to both audio and MIDI clips. Clip start and end markers can now be separated from the length of a clip's loop, so a clip can start playing one-shot style, then 'run into' a loop. Whenever that clip is retriggered, it will begin playing from the offset start marker. There are 'set' buttons for loop position, length, and clip start and end markers – these buttons are MIDI assignable, so you can go quite deep into loop manipulation from a keyboard or hardware controller.

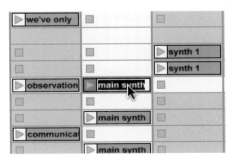

Renaming a clip

Nudge controls

(Right) Nudge controls with MIDI mapping

Nudge

New in Live 5, the Nudge buttons allow you to jump through a playing clip in increments the size of the global quantization period. It was already possible to play with a clip's offset values, but the nudge controls make it a lot easier. Nudging can be mapped to MIDI or computer keyboard control – forwards, backwards, revert (dumps nudge offset), and keep (moves Clip Start Marker to current offset position). An extra control can be MIDI mapped – Clip Scrub Control; assign a continuous controller knob to this for free scrolling backwards and forwards. Nudge mapping is global, not clip-dependent: you don't have to assign separate controllers for every clip you want to nudge.

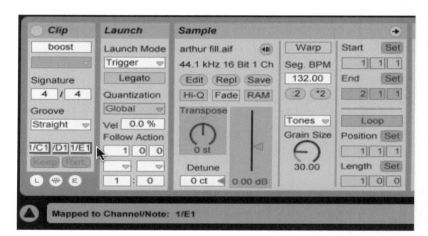

(Below) A 'nudged' clip – dot indicating nudge offset

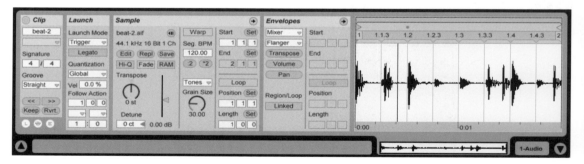

Groove

If you're used to working with MIDI sequencing, you'll be familiar with the concept of 'groove' – an attempt to humanise MIDI programming, this introduces slight offsets to note timing, just as a real instrumentalist might play a little off the beat. With Live (as of Live 4) you can apply groove settings to audio clips as well as MIDI clips – every clip has a Groove menu in the Clip View. The important thing to remember is that you have to set a Global Groove Amount in Live's control bar for clip groove to take effect.

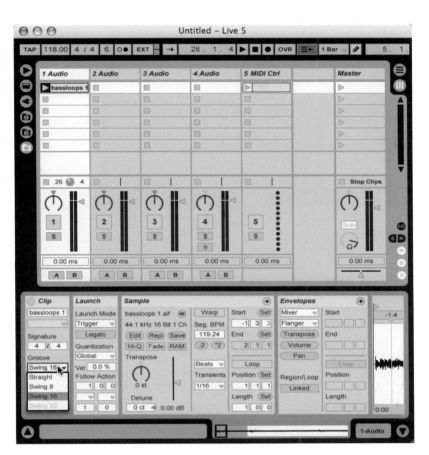

The clip groove popup menu shown at bottom right

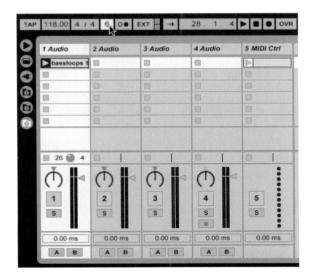

The global groove option

Unlinking clip envelopes

Clip envelopes – clip-level automation instructions – are effective enough, but Live 5 has added the ability to unlink envelopes from their 'host' clips; to set different loop lengths for the envelope than for the actual audio or MIDI note content. This means that clip automation envelopes can be longer or shorter than the actual clip they're attached to, giving the potential for some interesting creative effects and workrounds. You could use this technique to make a short clip fade in or out over a longer time, or to create changes to effects parameters, ie filter sweeps.

The audio clip before unlinking

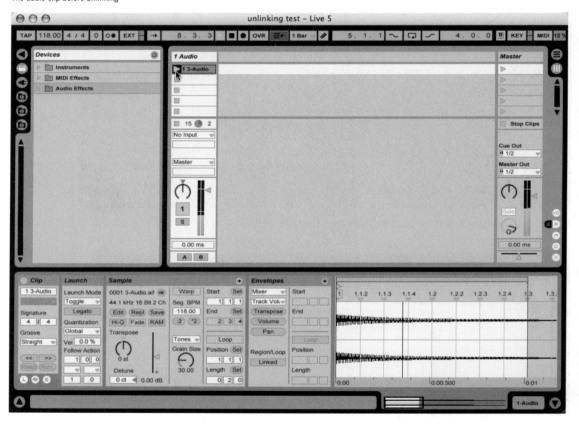

- What I most like about this is that different envelopes on the same clip can be linked or unlinked independently, and have different lengths assigned to them. In the screenshots I've got a 2-beat audio clip looping, with a 2-bar transposition envelope, and a 1-bar volume envelope. Sounds nice!
- If you want to seriously break the relationships between clips and their envelopes, you could turn off grid snapping, so you can draw in envelopes that don't conform to the nearest 'proper' subdivision of a bar/beat.
- Don't get confused – remember you have to unlink every individual envelope that you want to work with.

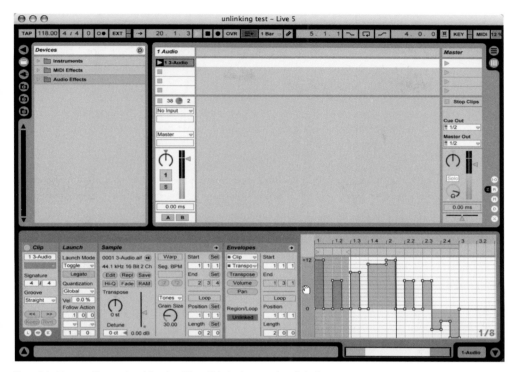

The unlinked transposition envelope (above) and the unlinked volume envelope (below)

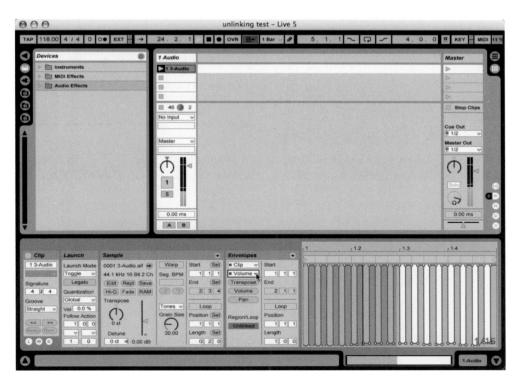

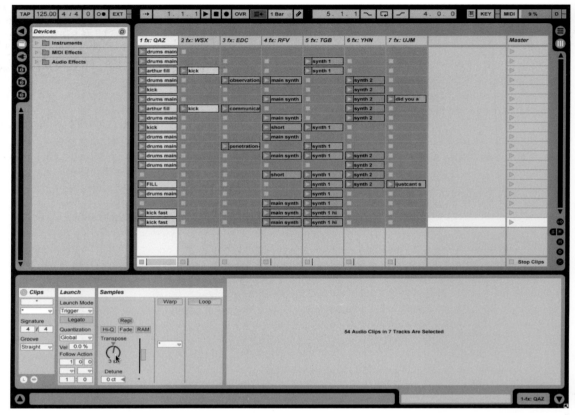

Transposition of multiple audio clips

Some of the housekeeping clip things are incredibly useful – see Chapter 8 'Performance Notes' for some talk about colour-coding and naming clips, and 'What's New' for information about multiple clip selection. If you select several audio clips at once, or even all of the audio clips in your set, you can transpose them together, by the same amount – kind of a global transpose workround, if you need to transpose your entire song. If you include any MIDI clips in this selection though, the transpose control won't be available!

Consolidation

If you've been bugging Ableton for an audio editor just because you want to trim clips, then leave them alone; there is a way, when you're working in the Arrangement View. Got a clip you want to trim? Drag the edges of the clip until it plays just the piece of audio you want to hear. Zoom in to get a higher editing resolution if necessary. Use Ctrl-j/cmd-j or 'Edit/Consolidate', a short progress bar will appear, and a new audio file will be created, containing only the chosen chunk of the original. If you're using a self-contained set, Live will prompt you to discard the original version of the clip when you close the set. Does that count as editing? Think so. It's a philosophical thing – if you're used to working with audio editors, then you need to adjust to this way of doing things.

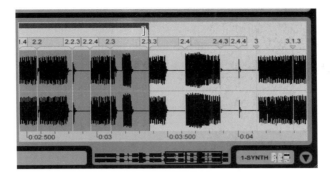

Using the loop bracket to select part of an audio clip

- Clips must be in Arrangement View for consolidation. For clips in Session View, click-hold on the clip, hit tab, then drop it into the Arrangement View. Consolidate it, then click-hold-tab it back into Session.

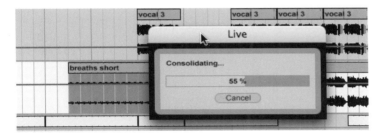

Consolidation in progress

- Consolidation takes place before Live's effects stage, so they're not rendered with the clip. However, any warping, gain, or transposition changes are incorporated.
- Remember you can also split clips in the Arrangement View – which can be useful alongside consolidation.

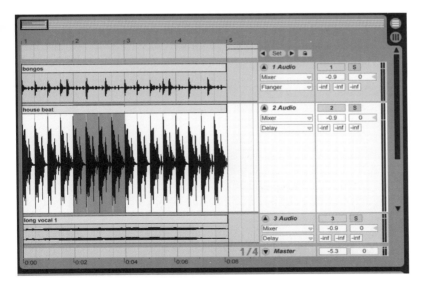

Taller track view

- Create a more 'editor-like' appearance in Live by dragging a Live track taller, and zooming in for a closer look.
- Consolidate won't create an audio clip from a MIDI clip, although you can consolidate a MIDI clip to create another. To create an audio clip from a MIDI clip, solo the track it's on, select the MIDI clip, and render to disk, or record the MIDI clip's output to an audio track.

Clip deactivation button – shown bottom left

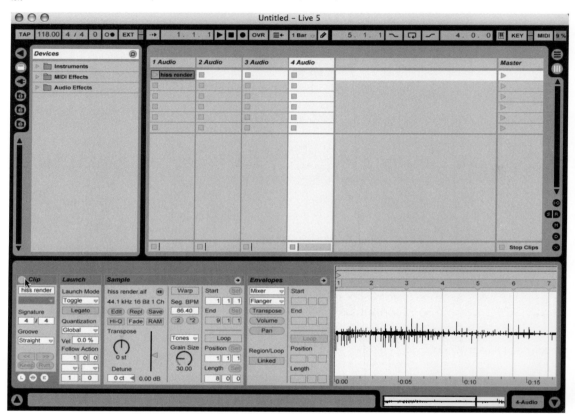

- If you've got a clip or clips you want to deactivate temporarily, for some reason, there's now a button just for you, next to the word 'Clip' in the Clip View window. You can also deactivate clips from the main menu or context menu.

Follow actions rule!

Follow actions do rule, it's true. While the idea of a set of clips that randomly trigger themselves may seem like you're letting the software do the talking, nothing could be further from the truth. There are so many ways to set up follow actions, so many things you can do with them, that you always feel in control. Sure, if you want to just do robot music you can, but it's your choice. If you haven't explored follow actions yet, you should try them now; they're hours of fun – again, that game-like quality appears.

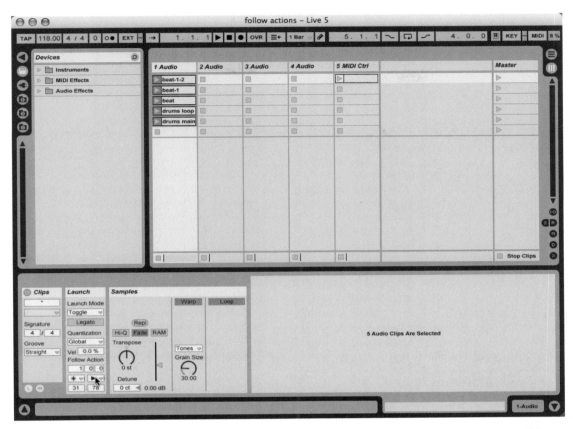

Multiple clip assignments of follow actions

- You can use Live 5's ability to select multiple clips to assign follow action behaviours to blocks of clips at once.
- Follow actions will be included in any recording that you do, just as if you triggered each clip yourself.
- Create hundreds of short (less than a bar, but not all the same length) clips, spread them across three or four tracks, and have parallel streams of follow actions, crossing over each other at unpredictable points. Throw in some delay too – things can get quite hypnotic.
- Use follow actions to provide some unpredictable changes in your beats when jamming along with an instrument.
- Use follow actions to perform 'utility' tasks in your live sets, like maybe at the end of a song, where you have one long clip which fades over 8 bars, and you have other shorter looping clips which you want to stop earlier, sometime during that 8 bars.
- Follow actions are a key part of the process described in Chapter 7 'Live Talks To Itself'. Thanks to ReWire (and the IAC Bus for OSX users, and – hopefully – MIDI Yoke for XP users), you can do crazy stuff with MIDI clips and follow actions.

Live clips

Live Clips can be MIDI or audio clips, but they're not the same as plain old Session View clips; they're a new way of saving clips for use in future projects, independent of the Live set they originated in. To create, one, just drag it from Session View to the Browser, and – if you like – rename it. This saves the original clip, plus all clip and envelope settings, and any devices used in the original track. If you're working on a new (empty) Live track, dragging in a Live Clip will add the

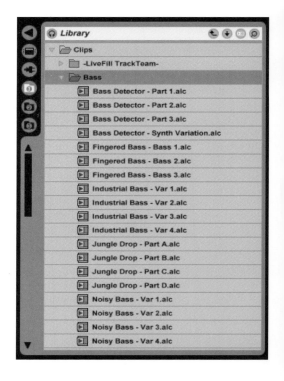

necessary devices. If you're working on a track that already includes devices or other clips, then the devices won't be loaded.

• Live Clips don't contain a copy of the original sample file – you could create a ton of Live Clips based on one audio clip.

Audio clips

When Live began, audio clips were all it had. They've come a little way since then (not a long way, because they were pretty much right first time). Many of the points to make about audio clips relate to other things mentioned in this book – every chapter has something that's relevant to audio clips, so I'm not going to repeat it all here.

Live 5 introduces the Complex warp mode; which is especially useful now that people are likely to be dragging entire songs into their Live sets as MP3s, as well as being yet another DJ-friendly function. This is a warp mode that accommodates mixed source material, so if you're use a drum loop you'd use Beats, for a keyboard part you'd use Tones, and for a song or part of a song comprising drums, bass, guitar, and vocals, you'd use Complex.

Auto-warping is a huge time-saver – long clips are automatically warped as they're imported; from what I've seen so far Live does a good job of identifying and calculating these – especially for more straight-ahead music, you'll probably find that Auto-Warp gets it right first time. If not of course, you can still edit the markers yourself. You can also pre-warp songs/long clips by choosing 'Analyze' in the File Browser context menu. That way the song will be available for play as soon as you drop it into a Live set (otherwise it takes a little while for songs be available while they're being auto-warped). If you don't want auto warping to take place, you can disable it in Preferences/Defaults.

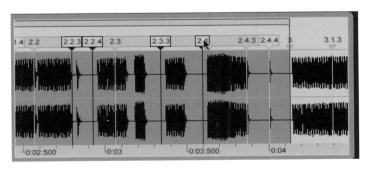

• It's possible to add warp markers to playing clips.

LIve's metronome is very useful as a clinical no-doubt-about-it arbiter of time when you're working with a loop and its start/end points or warp markers. Click on the symbol in the control bar. Use the Cue Volume control to change the metronome volume.

(Above) The metronome

(Left) The metronome volume control

• Shift-click on several warp markers to move them at once, retaining their relative spacing.
• You can divide and trim audio clips in Live, it's just not done in the usual way. Read about Consolidation, above.

Selecting multiple warp markers

The save clip button

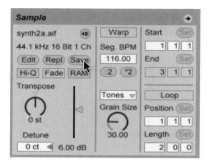

- A little reminder: there's a small Save button in Clip View, which attaches the current clip settings to the relevant audio sample (as part of the .asd file). Whenever you use this clip again in a Live set, the same settings will be applied.

MIDI clips

I love working with Live's MIDI clips – they do such a good job of integrating MIDI with audio, it's totally fluid. If you're coming at it from MIDI hardware grooveboxes, you won't have any trouble relating to it. If you're coming from Pro Tools or Logic, it may take you a bit longer, but the changes are all good! How you create MIDI clips is up to you. I'm not a keyboard player, and after years of working with MIDI sequencers, I find Live is so comfortable to use that I'm happy to just draw in notes with the pencil tool; it doesn't get in my way at all.

Showing 'record quantization' menu item

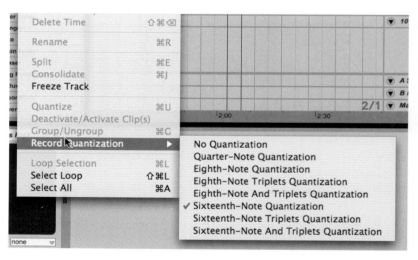

However, if you do like to enter notes in real-time, then Live 5 has some useful quantization tools. Select record quantization in the edit menu, and choose from a list of options ranging from no quantization, through eighth-note quantization, to sixteenth-note and triplets quantization. Any real-time MIDI note recording you make after this change will reflect this value, until you change it again.

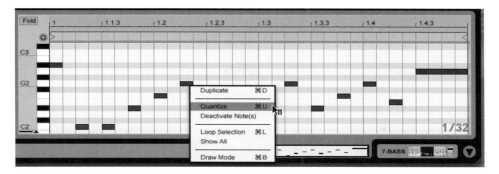

You can also apply quantization to recorded MIDI notes after the event, by selecting the note or notes and choosing Quantize from the edit menu, forcing them to conform to your previously selected value, or use Ctrl-u/cmd u to bring up a dialog box with more detailed quantize options, such as the resolution, adjust note start/end, and amount – the amount setting is quite useful if you want to retain any human feel to what you've recorded; instead of rigidly applying strict quantization to get a robotic feel, it'll apply the rules to a selected percentage, which can help retain some organic qualities..

The MIDI note quantization menu

Use the contextual menu to view a list of resolution options for the MIDI clip grid, based upon two types of grid – adaptive (display varies according to level of zoom), and fixed (divisions remain constant).

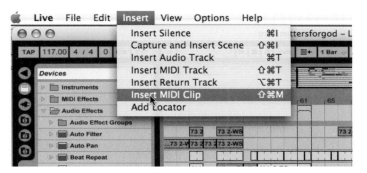

The 'insert MIDI clip' menu item

• You can't click to create a MIDI 'clip' in the Arrangement View (like you can in Session View), but you can drag to highlight an area, then choose insert midi clip from the menu, or Shift-ctrl-m/Shift-cmd-m.

Live 5 introduces a Preview switch in the MIDI Editor, another addition that is common to DAWs – whenever you enter, or click on, or move, a note in a MIDI clip, you can hear it too!

Now you can deactivate notes within a MIDI clip. If for some reason you want to temporarily 'kill' a couple of notes within a clip, this is the way to do it. I sometimes use this when I'm creating variations on an existing MIDI part. I'll copy the clip, then deactivate the portion that I want to change. That way I can draw in the new notes while keeping the original part as a visual reference.

As well as creating MIDI parts from scratch, Live can import MIDI files created elsewhere (the web is full of them). A MIDI file appears as a folder in the File Browser; each track within the MIDI file appears separately inside the folder; just drag them into Live as usual.

- You can preview MIDI clips in the File Browser, just like audio clips – you'll hear them with the correct instrument sound, even if you haven't loaded the instrument into your Live set yet.

Exporting MIDI from Live isn't so tidy – you can only export individual MIDI clips, there's no way to save a type 0 or type 1 MIDI file containing all the MIDI tracks in your set. I guess if you've built a lot of MIDI tracks in the Arrangement View, you could export them individually and re-assemble in another sequencer. Looped MIDI clips will only export as one-shots – although you could consolidate them first. The other way to do it would be to send MIDI via ReWire to another sequencer, like Reason, and record it in real-time. Doing anything like that in real-time seems ugly these days, but it's better than nothing!

Scenes

When you want to trigger a bunch of clips simultaneously, you put them in a horizontal row and trigger that from the right-hand (master) track. These rows are called scenes. You can construct a Live set in Session View, and spend your performance simply clicking your way vertically through the scenes. If this is all you do, it's pretty low-maintenance; maybe a bit too easy.

A scene – highlighted horizontal row

(Left) Scene select MIDI assignments

(Right) scene bpm

But if you use this as the basis of your set and add some one-shots, effects control, some freewheeling unstructured sections – why not?

There are several different ways to trigger scenes. You got your basic clicking, as I mentioned above, but you can also assign a MIDI note or a character from your computer keyboard (you can trigger scenes via MIDI clips if you read Chapter 7 'Live Talks To Itself!'). When you enter Key Map Mode or MIDI Map Mode, scene-specific controls appear at the bottom of the Master track – Scene Launch, Scene Up, Scene Down, and Scene Select (scrolling). I use the transport controls on the Ozonic to work with these; they'd also be great if you're playing an instrument, you could use the FCB1010 foot controller to scroll up and down through scenes.

Showing 'select next scene on launch' preferences item

Scenes can be used to trigger BPM changes, a feature which, when introduced, made a world of difference to performing with Live. All you have to do is name the clip something like '96 BPM'. You can type it in different ways: 96 bpm, 96 BPM, 96bpm, or 96BPM – they all work; BPM 96 doesn't work!

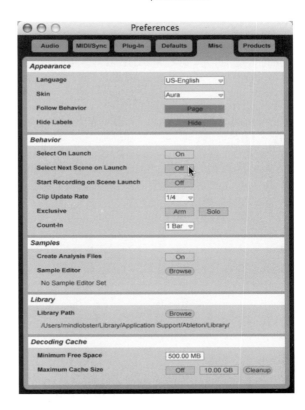

- If you've got a lot of scenes to name, do it fast: rename the first one as usual, then use the tab key to move on to the next instead of hitting 'enter'..

Scenes can be copied, pasted, deleted, and duplicated, like anything else. They have some other interesting characteristics: in Preferences, you can choose 'Select Next Scene on Launch', which enables you to move downwards through scenes just by pressing 'enter' or 'return'. If you choose 'Start Recording On Scene Launch', any armed clips in the launched scene will start recording.

'Capture and Insert Scene' MIDI item

Insert Scene	⌘I
Capture and Insert Scene	⇧⌘I
Insert Audio Track	⌘T
Insert MIDI Track	⇧⌘T
Insert Return Track	⌥⌘T
Insert MIDI Clip	⇧⌘M
Add Locator	

- Capture and Insert Scene is one that I always try to remember. It copies all playing clips in the current scene into a new one immediately below, very handy for when you're working on song structures.

In case you're wondering, you can't save scenes with BPM info to the Library, as such. You can drag a row of clips in the Browser, and they'll be saved, but it doesn't save the scene name or BPM settings. You could take advantage of a new Live 5 feature: create a Live set containing just the BPM scene, and drag that into the Browser, then drag that back into whatever set you want to use it in. I can't see any use for this at the moment, but maybe something will come up!

Scenes are an essential part of using Live's Session View – they relate equally to live performance and songwriting.

Song header scenes

In 'Performance Notes' I described how to build a Live set that contains several songs, arranged vertically in the Session View, and I talked about the importance of labelling and colour coding. Another useful thing is to create a header that divides the songs (visually), and makes room for some useful labelling – a line drawn across the Live set, with the song name, and any other info that might be useful, like reminders of BPM or channel changes.

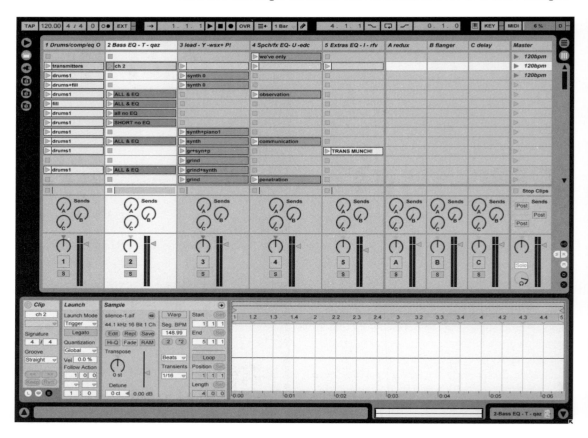

The first thing you have to do is create a silent audio clip. You can do this by creating and arming an empty audio track, selecting another track (where nothing's playing) as an audio source, and hitting record, then trimming the resulting clip to 1 bar in length. Then copy it, colour it, and label it as necessary – see screen shot at foot of previous page; I use yellow for my headers. These don't send any info or play any sounds; they're just visual guides.

Routing audio between tracks
Here's that little bit on tracks promised in the chapter title…

Sending audio to return tracks
For every Return track that you create – Ctrl-alt-t (PC), cmd-alt-t (Mac) – Live adds a Send knob to the relevant track. If you've got a Return track with an audio effect on it, you can share that effect over several tracks – very CPU efficient. It's usually best to set the effect's dry/wet control all the way to wet, using the track's Send knob to control the amount of effect. Return tracks have no Input slots, but they do have Outputs – their output can be re-routed to other tracks rather than directly to the Master track.

Audio from one track to many
You can send the audio output from one track to several others simultaneously (this includes the audio from MIDI tracks that have instruments assigned). You could put different effects on every track, pan them differently, send some to a return track, mess with their volumes, put a Gate or EQ on them – and of course record it all. Just select the 'source' track in the Input Type slot for each 'target' track.

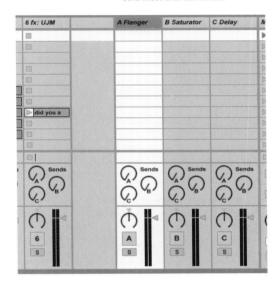

Send knobs and return tracks

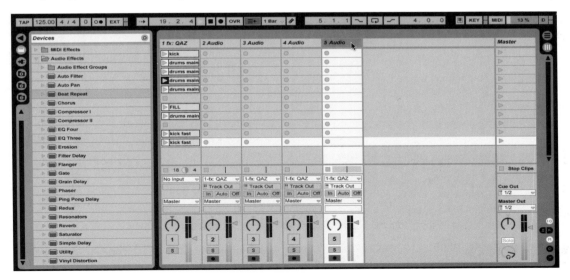

Audio routed from one track to many

This feature is built into the Impulse drum sampler – you can choose each separate Impulse slot as an input source for other audio tracks.

- Remember to arm the track to hear the incoming audio.
- Don't get confused between recording audio or MIDI and automation; audio won't be recorded to your drive until you hit the record button in a clip slot on each track.
- This kind of routing also works with audio from an external source, like a microphone or Reason.
- You could begin a performance with an empty set, record a short piece of audio, such as the room sound, then have fun routing it around various tracks, sends, and effects.

Audio from many tracks to one

Turn that on its head, and send the audio from several tracks to one. This is a way of re-sampling Live's output, or part of it, at any time, to further manipulate within the song. Choose the 'target' track in the Output Type slot for each 'source' track.

- Combine the two approaches: send one track to many, and simultaneously route some of the 'many' back to another single track.
- If you're recording from outside sources and have live microphones involved, watch out for feedback – remember the monitor In/Auto/Off options.
- Create a sub mix, pre-mixing selected tracks to one, before sending it to the Master output. This lets you put the fader and pan and effect settings for several tracks at the disposal of one control for each function.

Audio routed from many tracks to one

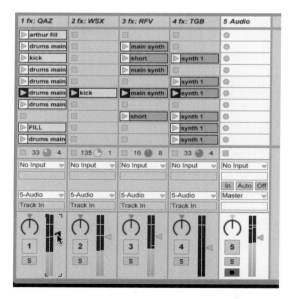

It works with MIDI too – from one track to many

Create a MIDI clip in a new track, with some notes and/or controllers – don't add any instruments to the track. That way you'll see MIDI outputs instead of audio outputs at the bottom, and you can send those MIDI notes all over the place. Choose your 'source' MIDI track as the Input Type for each 'target' track, and arm them for recording, then add your chosen software instruments/MIDI effects for each track.

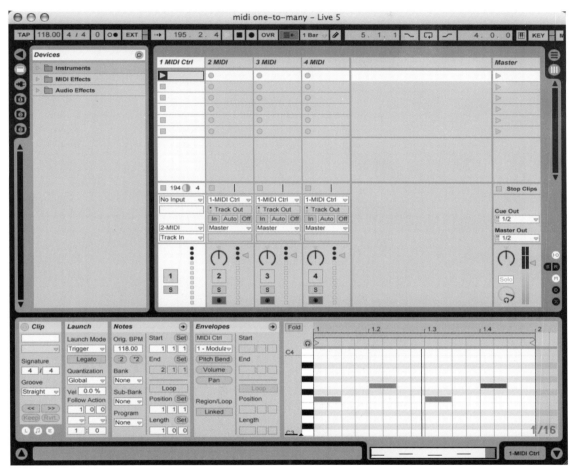

MIDI routed from one track to many

- Send the same MIDI part to two or three different instruments at once to layer sounds.
- You can also send MIDI controllers.
- Check your channel numbers. A single track can only send MIDI on one channel at a time!

Sending MIDI from many tracks to one

And again...choose the 'target' MIDI track in the Output Type slot for each 'source' track, and arm the 'target' for recording.

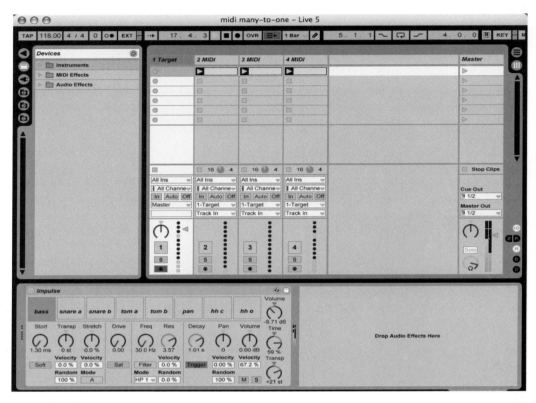

MIDI routed from many tracks to one

(Opposite page above) MIDI bounced from many tracks to one – part 1

(Opposite page below) MIDI bounced from many tracks to one – part 2

- Remember not to add software instruments to the 'source' tracks, or they'll default to sending audio instead of MIDI.
- Create percussion parts with a separate track for each percussion instrument, then send them all to Impulse on the 'target' track.
- You can bounce multiple MIDI tracks to a new single MIDI track, just like with audio. You don't need any instruments assigned to any of the tracks. This is a good way to create a new instrument part from others – I've done this before, combining two different bass parts; on a song of my own, and on somebody else's during a remix.

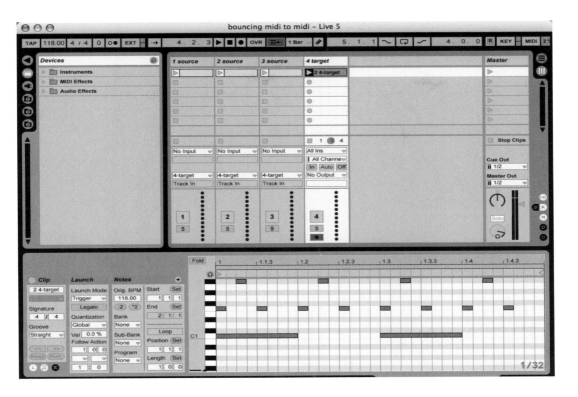

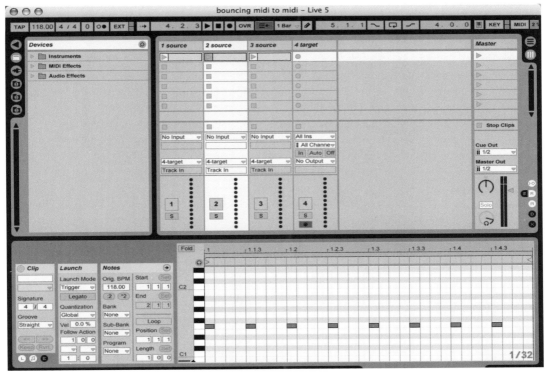

Devices

Live's 'native' plug-ins are divided into three categories: Instruments, MIDI Effects, and Audio Effects. There are three Instruments (as long as you paid for the Operator upgrade – more on that later), six MIDI Effects, and twenty-two Audio Effects. You can use third-party Audio Units and VSTs with Live, but get familiar with the bundled items first. The Live Device interfaces follow the trusted Ableton principles – very functional, but with a touch of style; they're all mappable via MIDI or the computer keyboard, and their presets can be accessed via the new improved Browser/Library.

Audio effects

Live 5 introduces five new Audio Effects: Flanger, Phaser, Saturator, Auto Pan, and Beat Repeat. Flanger and Phaser are the least interesting of these (in the nicest possible way), more a matter of adding something that 'ought' to be present, rather than innovation. According to Ableton they're modelled on 'classic '70s guitar effects'. Having said that, Phaser does have some great presets, which illustrate the wide potential of this effect – compare the Dischord and Great Buddha presets.

Saturator, like Flanger and Phaser, is a functional addition, bringing a wider range of distortion options than were previously available with the Vinyl Distortion device, with an emphasis on added 'warmth' – possibly for use with guitar sounds. Don't be put off by this 'warmth' talk though; Saturator can be very destructive when you want it to be!

Auto Pan? It's in the name; it creates subtle or not-so-subtle shifts in the left-right balance. I've used auto pan effects a lot, in software and hardware, it's a great way to bring a part to life. Ableton's incarnation allows you to set a rate manually, or to sync to project tempo. It also goes beyond regular 'pan' type sounds, and can create some nasty chopped-up beats.

(Above) all of Live 5's devices

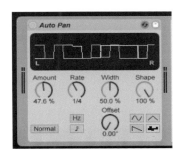

Saturator and Auto Pan

Beat Repeat – sounds great with non-rhythmic material

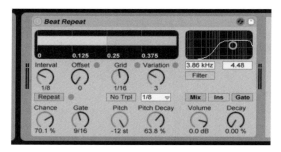

Beat Repeat is quite understated in a way – somehow I didn't pay much attention to it at first. That changed over time though – Beat Repeat rocks! Once again, the presets do a good job of illustrating what this effect is about. Don't be misled by the name, though – Beat Repeat sounds great with non-rhythmic material. The features to mess with most are Pitch, Pitch Delay, and Gate – this only feeds out the processed portion, which can be used if Beat Repeat is on an return track, but also can sound cool on a regular track...

Info – overlooked plug-in of the week

Utility, in the Audio Effects folder, does some simple but handy jobs around the Live house. It has controls for mute, gain, and stereo width (right down to mono), and it also lets you invert the phase of either channel. Clicking either the L or R buttons will send the left or right channel to both outputs – use this if you have a stereo file, and you only want to process one channel.

MIDI effects

Ableton are slowly adding MIDI effects – Live 5 brings only one new arrival in this field, but it's a good one – the Arpeggiator. The arpeggiator is an essential tool for anybody after a '1980s' sound; this one does that retro thing well, but with more flexibility than you'd get from the hardware synths and sequencers of old.

The Hold function is what it's all about. The Arpeggiator will keep playing the current pattern until you play some other notes. If you're still holding down the original notes, and you add more notes, they will be added and held too. Hit a note that's already held to release it. You can change the Style (direction of the notes, ie up & down) while Hold is active.

You can apply any of Live's MIDI Effects to external software or hardware via ReWire, just like sending other MIDI info – just drop them into a MIDI track with some clips, but without an instrument.

Instruments

Live includes three instruments – that is, as I mentioned earlier, as long as you paid for the optional Operator synth. These instruments, like the Audio and MIDI Effects, have all the advantages that you'd expect from Live-native devices; a consistent interface, and integration into the rest of the Live universe.

The two default Instruments are Impulse and Simpler. They're variations on a theme, being alternative ways of dealing with sampling – in some ways they don't do much different from Live clips, but – as when I first started using Live to organise QuickTime loops – they repackage it in a much more efficient way. The entire Live application itself is like a giant sampler anyway, so you can think of Impulse and Simpler as being samplers within a sampler; microcosms of what Live does on a larger scale, rather than software samplers in the vein of EXS or Halion. Dragging and dropping of samples is at the heart of them. You can drop in a sample from the Browser, or an audio clip, or your computer desktop, and start triggering it immediately. This is almost toy-like simplicity compared to some other sampling systems, but it doesn't lack for tweaking options and creative potential.

Impulse's drag'n'drop friendliness encourages you to create 'kits' that combine sounds of all types

When I first looked at Impulse, I was a little confused. I'd been using Reason to create drum parts for some time, and I was expecting the slots in Impulse to somehow correspond to steps in a sequence. Once I realised that Impulse was kind of a blank sample playing instrument, and it interacted with MIDI clips like any other, then – no problem. Live's collage philosophy comes into play at instrument level too – Impulse's drag'n'drop friendliness encourages you to create 'kits' that combine sounds of all types; of course you can save these kits in the Library for future re-use (don't forget to save a self-contained set if you want to transfer your set to another computer). The most fun part with Impulse is the fact that each of the eight loaded sounds can be treated totally independently. Even better, each sound can be assigned to a separate audio output, for wild routing games. See 'Clips And Scenes...' for more information on routing audio and MIDI in Live.

Quote

'I love the way the Simpler works. Just drag an audio file from anywhere (the arrangement, a folder), and drop into the plug-in, it's so simple and quick.' – *Jody Wisternoff (Way Out West)*

If you're routing one of Impulse's outputs to another audio track for effects processing, you don't need to record it as audio on that second track before you render your song – it will be included anyway, with – of course – the effects in place.

One of the few things I used Reason for was its retro style drum machine; now I use Impulse for everything – as long as I can find the kit sounds I want. Logic has a great new drum machine, called Ultrabeat, and there's no reason why that can't be used with Live via ReWire, but – again – it's not nearly so intuitive, and graphically so different from Impulse, that established Live users will feel far more at ease using Ableton's own drum machine.

Simpler – a very easy way to grab and start using a particular sound

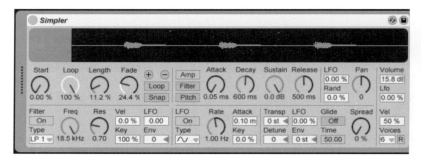

Simpler – well, it lives up to the name. Drag'n'drop, just like Impulse; it's quite like working with one of Impulse's eight sounds. It's not a monster sampler in its own right, but as part of the larger Live picture, it works great – a very easy way to grab and start using a particular sound as a sample for playing keyboards or drawing into MIDI clips. Don't be put off if Simpler sounds a little flat in isolation – the presets really come to life when they're used with MIDI or audio effects.

Operator is the one you have to pay for. It's Ableton's first synthesiser. Is it worth buying? Yes – for the quality sounds, and for the Live design continuity. To be honest, most of my time with Operator is spent with the presets – I'll use a preset, then work with EQ, effects, and resampling to change the nature of the sound. Live 5's Lessons give Operator thorough coverage, showing you how to create bass, percussion, lead, or pad sounds – Ableton are obviously eager to make sure we appreciate this thing. The presets reflect this range of sound possibilities, including some interesting rhythmic patterns, so you can use it straight away, and figure out how it works later.

Device Groups

Live 5 introduces Device Groups – accessible in the Device Browser. These are presets which contain combinations of devices; they will load all the devices with their individual settings. They come in Audio and MIDI varieties – create your own Device Groups by selecting adjoining devices and choosing Group Devices from the Edit menu. You can crack open a device group at any time by choosing Ungroup Devices.

Some of the preset Device Groups are quite CPU-heavy, so you might need to call on track freeze when working with these.

Device delay compensation

Also new to Live 5 – device delay compensation. This is Live's way of dealing with the slight delay that can occur when an audio signal is input and then
comes out the other end – all tracks are kept in sync, and hopefully there is
little if any apparent delay between what goes in and what comes out. I've
found certain latency problems in Live 4 have disappeared in 5.

If you open a pre-Live 5 set, device delay compensation defaults to off,
and you'll have to activate it manually in the Options menu. Generally
Ableton recommend leaving this on at all times, but if you're having severe
latency problems when recording instruments, you could try turning it off.

If you're recording an external audio source like a voice or an instrument,
and running it through some of Live's audio effects, remember that it won't
'print' the effects with the performance unless you route the audio out from
the track with effects to another audio track, and record it there.

Audio recording with effects

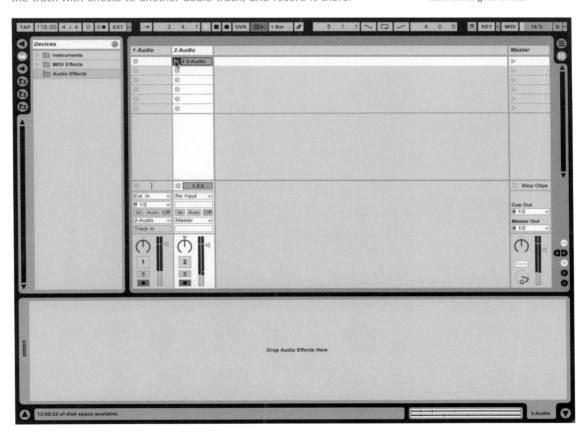

Vintage Warmer

It may seem funny when Live is such a blatantly 'electronic' instrument, but sometimes you crave more 'human' qualities. This is reflected in several different areas of Live use, the groove quantization features being the main example. Another area where this can be a concern is in processing, where subjective 'warmth' is a desirable thing. Reason has recently added the M Class Mastering Suite, which trades heavily on punch, clarity, volume, and sweetness – attributes which are considered to be very desirable, and to make your song sound like a 'proper' recording.

At the time of writing Live doesn't have anything like this as an integrated device, but there are other plug-ins that you can use. PSP AudioWare's Vintage Warmer EQ plug-in is a popular choice; this will make your Live sets sound better than spending the same amount of cash on an 'effect' plug-in, or sample CDs, or yet another 'ultimate' MIDI controller. Vintage Warmer contains 31 pre-sets, with something for every occasion – individual instrument tracks or entire mixes can get the treatment. It's available in VST/AU/DX formats, so it's Mac and PC compatible. You can of course save your own presets. Recently I've been using 'multi band comp limit light' across the mix on everything. I've saved it into my Live template, so I don't even think about it any more, I only notice it if I turn it off. This is a guaranteed way to add those magic sprinkles to your live set – volume, punch, warmth – aaahh, yes!

Download the Vintage Warmer demo and do some A/B testing through your regular speakers. You don't have to understand the mysteries of multiband mastering (which is good because I'd be in trouble), you can hear it working.

PSP AudioWare's Vintage Warmer EQ plug-in will make your Live sets sound better

Automation

Automation is what they call it when you record progressive changes to mixer or effects settings, so that the changes can be replayed or edited when the song is played back later. You're not 'burning' those changes into the audio of your song, the automation data (called envelopes) is recorded separately – it's non-destructive.

The 'what to click and where' aspects of automation are well-covered in the Live 5 manual. One thing to understand about automation in Live is that it happens at both clip and track levels, and it relates to the way that you can record and play back performances.

Pretty much everything can be automated in Live, except transport commands – you can get Live to stop itself, but you can't get it to start itself again (see Chapter 7 'Live Talks To Itself' for further explanation). It's easy to see which Live functions can be automated; hit Ctrl-m/cmd-m, for MIDI mapping, and any highlighted controls can be automated. Automation can be recorded in real-time, for example messages sent from a hardware controller during a performance, or it can be drawn in using Live's pencil tool. Of course, a bit of both is good – recording spontaneous movements with a hardware controller, then go through and edit them afterwards.

Clip automation in general

Exactly what you can automate at clip level depends on whether you're working with audio or MIDI clips. There are common things, however – the means by which information is entered are the same – use the pencil/Draw Mode, or click with the mouse to enter breakpoints, or record in real time. Any effect that's loaded in the same track as the clip can have its parameters automated, and the mixer parameters are always available – track volume, pan, and either transpose (for audio clips) or pitch bend (for MIDI clips).

Live 5's new clip nudge feature can also be automated – each 'nudge action' creates a new, quantized clip in the Arrangement View; see the screen shot overleaf.

There are various ways to automate clips and tracks. If you've got any parameters assigned to hardware controllers, then start recording, move that knob or fader, and everything you do will be recorded until you hit the spacebar or stop button. Otherwise, you can 'record' your automation without even entering record. This is because – of course (newbies note) – we're not recording audio here, just the controller movements. While your clips or tracks are playing, just draw the automation in.

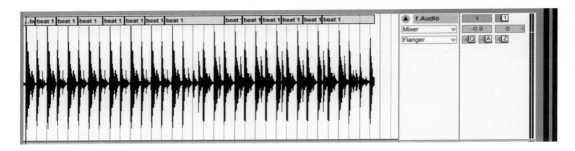

MIDI clip automation

When it comes to automating MIDI clips in particular, you can automate parameters for the mixer as usual (plus send levels for any send effects), software instruments, and any audio effects in line after the instrument. If you don't have an instrument on the track, you can send MIDI controllers to other apps or hardware. You also have the option of sending MIDI Bank, Sub-bank, or Program changes. (See 'Using Live 5 With Other Software and Hardware' on sending MIDI to other applications.)

Audio clip automation

After a little while, you'll see how working with MIDI clips is a fragmented version of 'regular' MIDI sequencing, which has its roots in the 1980s (that's not to underestimate it, though). Audio clips are a different proposition, especially as regards clip automation – these are things that were impossible before. I'm talking about the amazing warp markers, the warp mode options, clip groove...even the transposition at clip level makes a world of difference – you can use it to really mess up drum beats, for example. Combine these features with the ability to separate automation envelopes from clip length, and you're going into unknown territory.

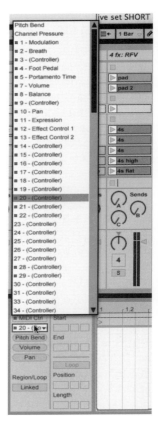

(right) MIDI controllers available with a MIDI clip

(below) Audio clip automation

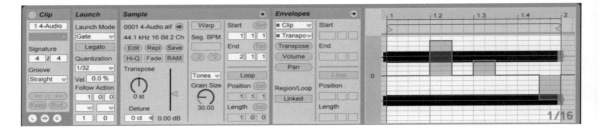

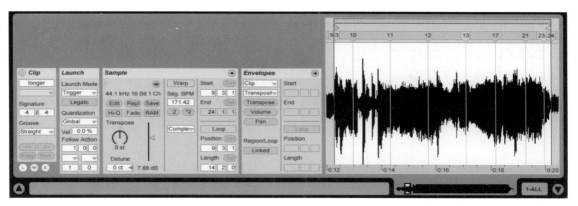

Here's an example of something I've done to an audio clip with warp markers and transposition envelopes; see the screen shots for more reference. I took a vocal sample from an old record, and trimmed it by consolidating the clip. This wasn't a clip that needed to loop; it was going to be a one-shot. I wanted the first half of the phrase to play at normal speed, then the second half to slow down as much as physically possible. I created a warp marker at the desired point, which was conveniently the start of bar 5. I then created more warp markers and dragged them around until the end of the clip (originally coming in at 5.3) was at the end of bar 24. When triggered,

Showing audio sample stretching in progress

Showing stretched audio sample with transposition automation

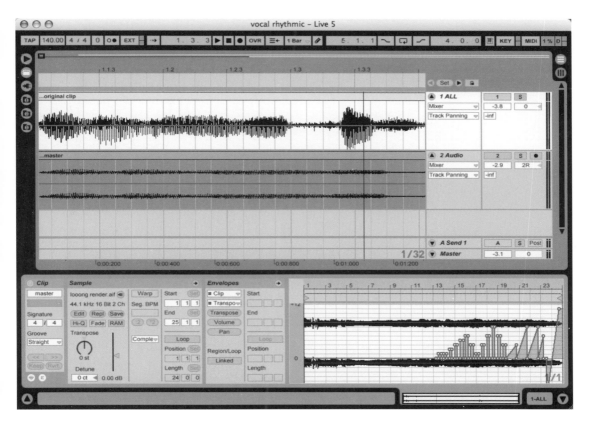

this clip would play at normal speed until it hit bar 5, then it would grind to an almost-halt. Then I got busy with the clip transposition envelope; see the screen shot for how it looked. This removed the last traces of humanity from the stretched clip, adding a creepy synthesised quality – which is a good thing.

Showing close up of transposition

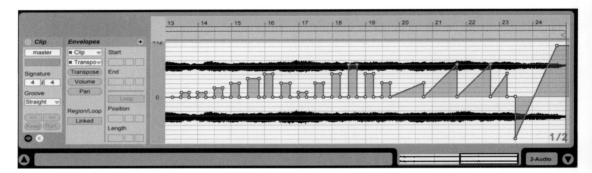

Clip info

Clip envelopes are 'burned in' to your new audio file when you consolidate a clip.

•

Clip envelopes aren't reversed when you reverse an audio clip. If you reverse a clip that fades out, it'll still fade out!

Automating the cross fader

Live's cross fader movements can of course be recorded during a performance, and edited (if necessary) later. The cross fader is interesting for non-DJs too – you can use it to create new beats and sounds, and the automation helps with this. Drop 3 different beats into a Live set – one beat per track. Add some other sound like speech on track 4. Assign some of the sounds to Deck A, and the rest to Deck B, play with the crossfader to see what happens, using either your mouse or a hardware fader/knob. Then record your cross fader moves in real time, or draw them in; this only needs to be over a couple of bars. Play it back – find a part that sounds good, then bounce it to another track, and use it as a fresh beat/loop.

Info

You don't have to be using beats for this – mix together any interesting sounds. You can also automate the A-B assignment, so a clip can jump decks as it goes on.

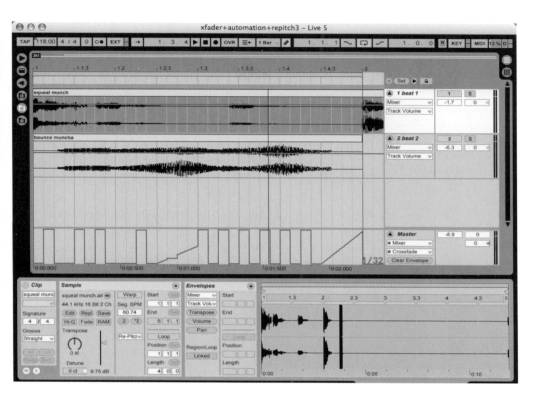

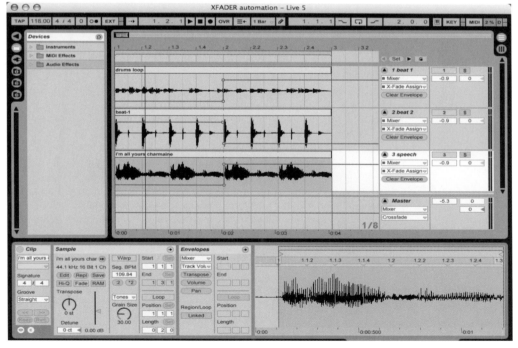

(Top) Crossfader automation   (Bottom) Crossfader 'deck' assignment automation

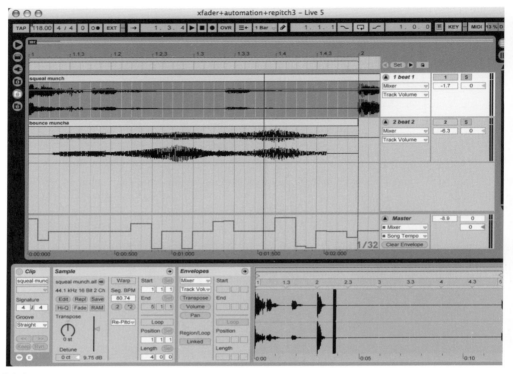

Showing crossfader/song tempo
automation

Go further: do a micro version, over one bar, using short noise loops, and
draw in a lot of fast crossfader assignments. Set the loops to Re-pitch, then
draw in some tempo changes over that bar. This can get quite messed up –
which is, yes, good.

Envelopes in tracks – the Arrangement View

Generally, using automation in tracks is the same as working in clips – drawing, editing, copying, etc. There's a useful 'Clear Envelope' button in the
Arrangement View mixer, and a 'Delete Envelope' command in the Edit
menu.

Info – the BTA button

You need to understand the Back To Arrangement button, in Live's Control Bar. Visible from either view, it
turns red when you depart from your recorded Arrangement – a track can't play an Arrangement and a
Session part simultaneously, and Session is prioritised. If you're playing back a song and something isn't
working like it should, click on this little fella and your problems will (should) go away!

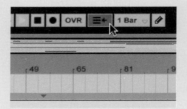

Versatile envelopes

Automation envelopes are really versatile, there's so many ways you can work with them:

- Copy an envelope you've drawn for one parameter, and paste it onto another, just to see what happens. You can also do this across different instruments and mixer functions.
- Click and drag around part of an envelope to move it to a new location. The remaining portion will stretch at the connection point.
- Use copy and paste to duplicate sections of an envelope, to save drawing in long/repetitive sections.
- You can copy an envelope from a track to a clip, and vice versa.
- Unlink an envelope from a looping clip so they can both run over different lengths, like 8 bars of clip automation on a 1 bar clip – if it's a suitable parameter, you'll hear a cumulative effect as the looping goes on.

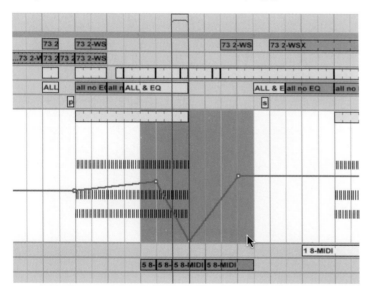

Selecting automation to copy

Envelopes in the Library

If you really enjoy drawing in complicated curves, you could create a folder in your Library for Live Clips with automation envelopes that you could reload and reuse; it's not unusual for Logic users to create 'favourite' envelopes that they use repeatedly.

Info

See the chapter 'Teaching Live' for more on experiments with automation envelopes.

•

See Chapter 7 'Live Talks To Itself' for some fun clip automation excess!

About the views

Left brain, right brain...

Take a seat, won't you – there's something we need to talk about, though I know I've mentioned it before. The relationship between the Session and Arrangement Views is a fundamental part of the Live experience, and you have to get to grips with it. Occasionally I run into people who work in only one View, and they're surprised when I mention what's possible in the other; it's very common that people who come to Live from Cubase or Pro Tools or whatever, gravitate to the Arrangement View, and just sit there – which is fine, but they won't be getting the most out of Live. Moving between Session and Arrangement requires nothing more than a tap of the tab key, and work-

Session View

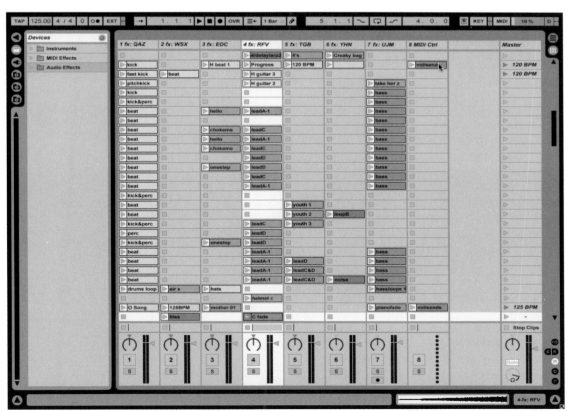

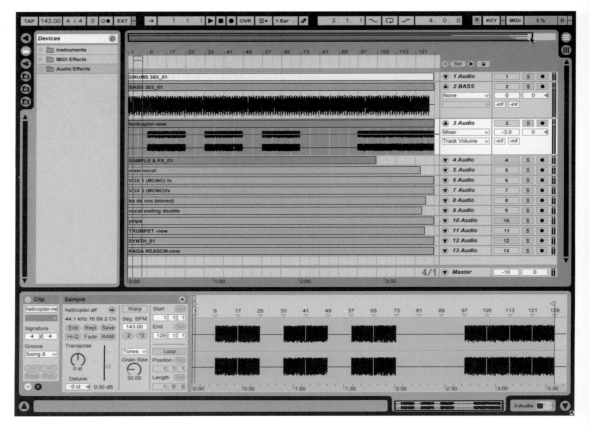

Arrangement View

ing in one doesn't mean you're forbidden from popping round the corner to visit the other.

Defining the Views can be a problem – not technically, but conceptually. Think of the two sides of the human brain – the left side is said to be the creative, spontaneous side, and the right is the practical, logical side. They work together in harmony to create a well-rounded, fully-functioning brain (er...on a good day). The Session View is Live's left brain – you can compile your audio material from various sources, drag'n'drop clips at will, experiment with crazy signal routings, make pretty musical patterns, arrange your clips into scenes, and jam around with intuitive song structures. Anything goes – this is Live as an instrument. The Arrangement View is Live's right brain. It's where you record and organise those improvised structures, add more automation, re-arrange parts, lay out your song's final arrangement, and mix in preparation for rendering the finished song. View your composition in a linear fashion, along a more 'traditional'-looking timeline ranging from left to right. Of course, you can still drag'n'drop new material, and perform tweaks and edits while Live is running, but it feels quite different from the Session View.

Session users might be surprised to hear that some people jam in the Arrangement View, which is just weird, although Live 5 has made this a lot easier – we'll get to that soon...

Live talks to itself

We all know how simple Live is to use. It's like a game – challenging you to make connections, to exceed the simplicity and do really strange things. One of these things is something I came across by mistake – and now I use it, I can't imagine it not being there, so it qualifies as useful and strange.

Live can send MIDI to itself.

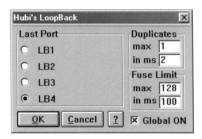

Hubi MIDI LoopBack

You can send notes or CC's from a MIDI track in Live, to all of the other tracks in Live. The principle is simple, and it's very obvious, although I haven't heard of anybody else doing it (and neither had Ableton at the time of writing). I'm sorry to say that once again Mac users have the advantage here – this is all about sending MIDI out from – and then back into – Live itself, something that's very easy to do with the IAC Bus in Mac OSX, but which requires third-party help under Windows XP; you could try something like Hubi's MIDI LoopBack or MIDI Ox. So far there are two major uses that I have for this, one very practical and the other quite crazy, and I'll detail them here. I'm not trying to tease you or give it a big build up, I just want to make sure I explain it clearly. And be careful – avoid getting into MIDI feedback where you have MIDI being sent and received by the same application – you can get into serious hang-ups!

Info – what is the IAC Bus?

The Mac OSX IAC Bus is something that you might never have encountered. 'IAC' stands for Inter Application Communication; if you remember OMS under Mac OS9, then – basically – this is it. Open Audio MIDI Setup in the Utilities folder, and click on the 'MIDI Devices' tab. You'll see icons representing various MIDI devices; ignore them and click on the icon for IAC Driver. In the resulting pop-up, make sure 'Device is online' is ticked, and there's at least one port in the list (you can create more than one port if you need it). That's all you have to do with the IAC – just make sure it's on! If you've made any changes, click 'Apply', then quit Audio MIDI Setup.

IAC Driver in Audio MIDI Setup

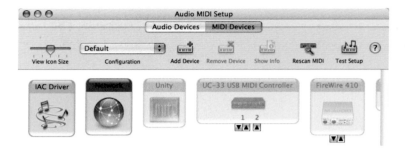

IAC properties

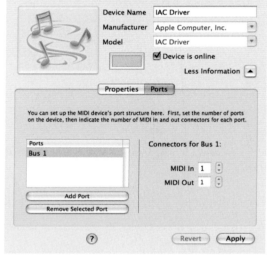

MIDI controllers being selected and edited in Live

Song setup clips

This is the most 'useful' of my two MIDI stunts. I use this method for every performance, and it's always worked fine, even when I'm simultaneously sending MIDI from Live to Arkaos VJ (via ReWire). The aim here is to create a MIDI clip to go at the top of each new song in a Live set. When triggered the clip will send 'jump to' messages to Live's mixer settings, in preparation for the next song – for example restoring all pans to the centre position; it's like loading a preset on a digital mixer. If you're working through a Live set that contains several songs, it means that one click sets you up for the next song – avoiding a lot of mousework.

As long as your IAC Bus

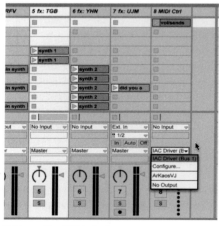

IAC Bus as Live MIDI destination

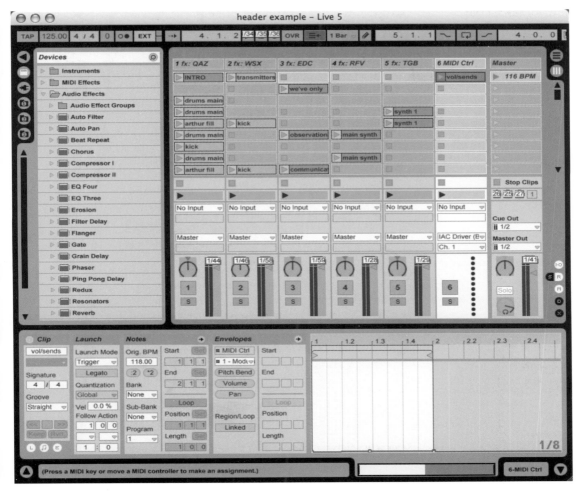

Setup clip at top right 'vol/sends', with relevant MIDI controllers selected throughout Session View.

is set up, it'll appear as an output destination beneath a MIDI track. Then go to Preferences and make sure the IAC Bus is listed as an Active Device in the MIDI/Sync tab. Select 'Track' and 'Remote' in both the Active Device Input and Output slots. Now any MIDI messages sent from your MIDI track will go in a loop courtesy of the IAC Bus.

Slight drawback: you need a MIDI hardware controller to map the MIDI controllers in Live in the first place. Once you've done that, you can then enter the necessary MIDI controller numbers and parameter changes in your Live clip – see the screen shot (left) for this, and see 'Automation'. It means that you can leave the hardware at home when you go out to play.

Another issue is that Live's built-in devices don't receive MIDI program changes, which is a shame, because then you could jump between totally different instrument sounds and effect settings between – or during – songs. It's also necessary to avoid sending too much MIDI information at the same time – as long as you're sending simple mixer resets, that should be okay. If you do run into any problems, try sending the MIDI info at slightly different times, or split it up to send on different channels.

Tip

Even when sending a '0' message, it's necessary to put in an incremental change, however small; otherwise Live doesn't pick it up.

Once you've got your 'reset' clip or clips sorted out, don't forget to drag them into the Library, so you can use them in future Live sets – the MIDI information will be stored as part of the Live Clip format. Remember to name them something useful! Even if you're using a hardware controller like the FCB1010 pedal board, or an Ozonic, this is still worthwhile, because it puts this 'reset' on one button or key.

The MIDI mangler

The aim here is to take this Live-MIDI-to-Live thing as far as it can go, but still to produce a usable result. My experience with the 'reset' MIDI clip led me to ask some new questions:

- Is it possible to combine this technique with follow actions to automate Live's clips to an extreme degree?
- Can Live be persuaded to play audio clips randomly, while also randomly changing mixer and effect parameters – and record the result without human intervention?

Session View with MIDI mapping visible

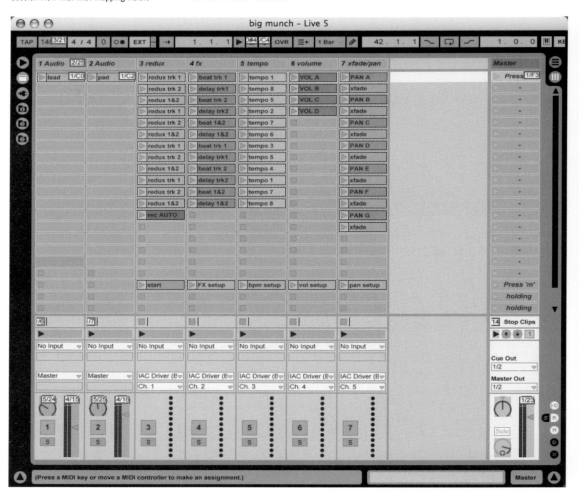

Of course the answer to these questions is 'yes', otherwise the paragraph above that would have been the end of this chapter. What I wanted to do was create a 'processor', based on follow actions and effects; something that would enable any two audio clips to be dropped in and mashed up, but which would produce different results every time; it's a work in progress, but this is where I'm up to.

First, all previous comments about Audio MIDI Setup and the IAC Bus apply. Then, refer to the screen shot of the finished article, it'll make the explanations a lot clearer. This Live set is based on the limitations of putting it together on my PowerBook; you might find that you can get it working on more, or fewer, simultaneous tracks, depending on your set-up.

- In Session View, I use two audio tracks, and five MIDI tracks.
- Each audio track has Redux, Beat Repeat, and Ping Pong Delay effects loaded.
- I mapped MIDI controllers to one function of each effect.
- I mapped MIDI controllers to the project tempo, the faders and pan pots of the audio tracks, and MIDI notes to the 'stop' and 'record' buttons.
- Each MIDI track contains a number of MIDI clips, each group of clips sending controllers to specific parameters. These include: Redux Downsample rate, Beat Repeat Chance, Ping Pong Dry/Wet Mix, tempo,

The finished article, with follow actions in progress

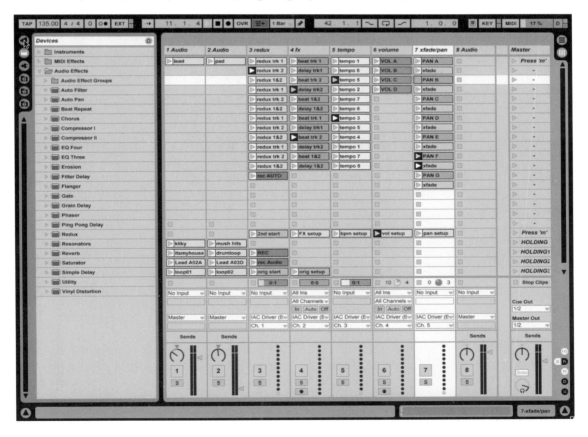

crossfade, and Track 1/2 volume and pan. Different clips in each MIDI track send different parameters, so the same parameters aren't being triggered over and over.

- I've applied follow actions to the clips in each MIDI track. I used the same settings for most of them: 'Any' and '50'; but in track 7 I used 'Next' to alternate between pan and crossfade.
- A few empty scenes below the follow action clips, I have a starting scene. This is similar to the MIDI 'song header' clips I mentioned earlier. The clips in this scene restore 'default' settings to the Live set. The leftmost clip 'start', sends a MIDI note to trigger the top scene in the Live set.
- I dropped one clip into the top slot of each audio track. It's important to prepare these clips properly – they must be set to 'loop', and the 'Re-pitch' warp mode should be selected.
- I mapped the letter 'm' to trigger my starting scene. When I press 'm', the MIDI note is sent to trigger the top scene, triggering the audio clips in the audio tracks, and the top follow action MIDI clips.
- That starts the thing off. As the follow actions trigger the MIDI clips, various MIDI controllers are sent. Effects parameters change, the mixer fades and pans automatically, and the entire 'song' speeds up and slows down.
- I saved the best until last; the final follow action clip in track one sends two MIDI notes – the first starts recording, and – one bar later – the second stops the entire track.
- This means that at a random point, this automated Live set starts and stops recording on its own; taking the whole process out of your hands.
- That's cool!
- Hit tab to go into Arrangement View, and look at what Live has recorded for you. At this point, disable all of the IAC outputs, so when you play back the recording, Live isn't still sending MIDI. Render it to disk as a separate file.
- I like this stuff – you can put in long or short clips, speech, beats, noises, instrument sounds; that's up to you. The Re-pitch setting is really important, because it works in tandem with the song BPM to drastically change the sound of the clips; instead of retaining their pitch as the song BPM changes, they 'speed up' and 'slow down', like vinyl.
- The record clip is the killer for me, but if you just want to keep it playing forever, just move that clip out of the follow action group. You could make longer recordings by creating longer record clips.
- Keep the new loops that you create by doing this; drop them into your future Live sets, and chop 'em up and warp them all over again!
- You might notice on the screen shot that each MIDI track sends on a different channel; an attempt to avoid clogging up channel 1.

Two clips go in one end, and come out the other end all mashed up! I hope this makes sense – it should at least give you ideas about things to try yourself. If Ableton could possibly build this automation into Live by simply allowing us to choose Live as a MIDI output/input, then it would be a little easier to implement, and would enable all Live users to create complicated structures.

Maybe you could use this in a performance situation, combining it with manually-triggered clips, and with the help of a hardware controller like the UC33e; though you'd have to make sure that your controller isn't sending on a channel that's already in use.

I have to say – try this at your own risk. I did find that Live got badly frozen up when I was trying to send too much info at once (no permanent damage done); that's why I settled on the layout seen here.

After this? It opens a lot of doors. The use of follow actions to 'time' a recording is quite interesting, don't you think? You can have huge cascades of MIDI clips and follow actions. I put this together before Live 5 was released; randomly-automated clip nudges will be included shortly.

This demonstrates what I've been saying about Live – it's like a game, building new connections from simple functions – whatever next?!

Build a 16-step sequencer in Live

If you've got a hankering for some retro-style step sequencing, but you don't have (or can't afford) the hardware, there is a way to do it in Live. This is a trick that you won't find anywhere else! Even better, unlike some of the other Live 'creations' described in this book, this one doesn't require any complicated MIDI routing, and is fully cross-platform.

It started when I was reading about hardware step sequencers, and I wanted to use Live 5 and my UC33 to emulate that experience; I came up with this solution. Here's how it works:

- Create a Live set with 17 MIDI tracks, and a return track with Ping Pong Delay.
- Load Simpler into track 1. Choose a preset with a suitable sound…bass or lead, that's your choice!
- Once you've got the Simpler sound the way you want it, save it as a preset called 'sequencer sound'.
- Now load Simpler into the next 15 tracks, and load the 'sequencer sound' preset in each.
- Track 17 is for drums – more on that later.
- Back to track 1 – create an empty 1-bar MIDI clip. Draw 16 adjoining notes of equal length, filling the bar.
- Select all of the notes except the first one, and deactivate them.
- Copy the clip across tracks 2 –16, and for each track activate the next note in the row, while deactivating the previous one.
- Now you have to do some MIDI mapping. Assign the UC33's faders 1– 8 to the first 8 faders in Live's mixer. Assign the first row of 8 knobs to Simpler's transpose control in each track. Assign the second row of knobs to Simpler's frequency control in each track. Assign the third row of knobs to the send knob for each track.
- For tracks 9 –16, you'll need to create a UC33 preset that sends on channel 2 (use Enigma to set this up); then assign the necessary MIDI controllers for those tracks, just like tracks 1– 8.
- Now, when you trigger the corresponding scene, the clips will begin playing together, but the 16 notes will play in succession, just like a step

Info

What is a step sequencer?

Step sequencers were the first sequencers around, in the days of hardware; using a deceptively simple structure – playing 16 (typically) notes, one after the other, in an endless loop, with parameters such as pitch being editable in real-time. It's amazing how much can be achieved with this simple arrangement. For modern hardware equivalents, take a look at Doepfer's products.

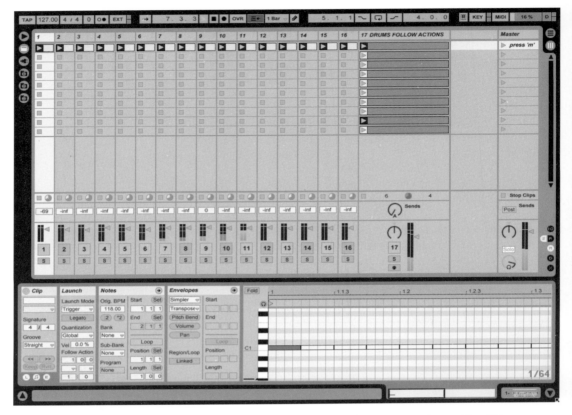

sequence! As long as your MIDI clips are set to loop, this will keep playing indefinitely, while you change the volume, pitch, frequency and fx send for each note.

- You can also use the computer keyboard to mute/solo individual tracks for more rhythmic interest.
- Assign fader 9 to song tempo.
- Load Impulse and some drum loops in track 17, and use follow actions to instigate a little random playback.
- Effects in the master track will make a lot of difference to the overall sound. To get the tone I wanted, I used (from left to right) Redux, Phaser, Saturator, and Compressor II.

Nearly everything you do with this setup sounds good...it's not exactly the same as using hardware, but it's close, and it has value in its own right. Hit record at any time and commit your sequencers to disk for later use.

Performance notes

Live is like one of those Transformers from the cartoons; in the studio it's a full-blown DAW, used for writing and production, then on stage it transforms into an instrument, with a very workable interface and real-time control over all functions. In a performance context, Live resembles the grooveboxes of old, but applying the philosophy to both MIDI and audio content in a way that hardware devices could only dream of (if they could dream). Yamaha came close, with their RM1x and RS7000, and their Motif range combines attributes of both of these, but they're different beasts from Live; they can't provide the same creative freedom.

The arguments about the validity of performing with computers are over, I think. Computers crash, guitar strings break, singers fall off the stage...I'd rather reboot my computer in front of an audience than re-string my bass – I know which would be faster too. And guitar-playing technophobes – a Les Paul is the product of vast amounts of industrial power; if you want true low-tech, go bang some sticks together.

If you're standing in front of an audience, and you're doing something where you have the potential to make great mistakes as well as great music – that counts as a performance.

A set for every song, or every song in the set?

Live users love to find the 'ultimate' way to do things – of course, there is no ultimate; in our field, things are changing constantly. Today's 'ultimate' audio interface is doomed to spend a lot of tomorrows getting dusty on the shelf, and a lot of day-after-tomorrows in the garage, with our MM-10s and QY10s.

One of our fruitless quests involves the construction of 'ultimate' Live sets for performance use – I guess you might call them Live live sets. There are so many ways to do this, and that's a good thing. The first thing to appreciate is that, although only one Live document can be open at a time, there's no need to have a separate Live set for every song. Even before Live 5, it was possible to have several songs structured vertically in one Session View, and use Live's BPM scene changes, channel changes from a keyboard/controller, and something like my Live song header idea – explained in Chapter 7 'Live Talks To Itself' – to work through the evening's set (DJs who like to work with an entire song per clip can disregard all of this).

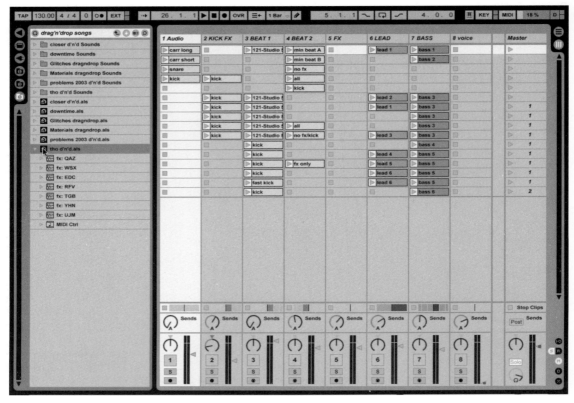

Live sets being dropped into each other

I say 'before Live 5', but all of this still works. What Live 5 adds is the ability to drag entire Live sets (or selected parts) from the File Browser into the current set. This is a fantastic development – it makes it much easier to mix and match songs, or parts of songs, and the adventurous spirit can go on stage with nothing on screen (or maybe an opening song), then drop in everything else from the Browser as the set progresses; you won't encounter any audio dropouts when you do this, but if you're dragging in a big set, there can be quite a wait for it to load, during which time you can't do anything in Live.

If you want to drag'n'drop sets into each other, you'll need a consistent structure for them – controller mapping, number of tracks, and effects used should remain constant, but many users stick to a common pattern in their performance sets anyway, saving the 'irregular' stuff for studio/home work/experimentation.

I work with a hybrid approach – I go on stage with most of my required songs loaded, but I also have a selection of 'spares' bookmarked in the File Browser, so I can go off on a tangent if I want to.

Prepare your set for performance

However you decide to build your set, there are things you can do to make it more performance-friendly.

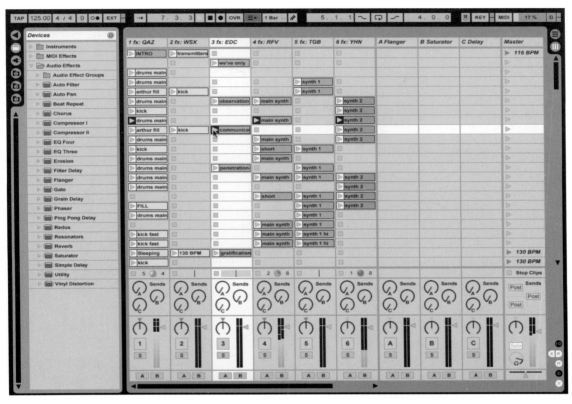

An example of the author's Live sets

- Pre render all software instrument clips – take the load off!
- Remember that you can now change the width of tracks in the Session View – spread them out to fill the available space and to make your clip labelling more visible.
- Consider lowering your screen resolution for on-stage use. What you lose in 'real estate', you gain in clarity. I used to do this, though I had to abandon it when I started ReWiring to Arkaos – just couldn't fit it all in!
- Label everything. Clips for sure, but the tracks too – I label mine with the letters that I need to trigger effects on that particular track. So if I have EQ and Beat Repeat on track 1, and Q and W will toggle those effects on/off, I name the track Q/W.
- Colour coding is helpful too – anything that gives you more information on screen at a quick glance. I have my own system- whenever I see a white clip, for example, I know it's a drum loop; blue is speech or vocals, etc.
- I set my global quantization to 1 bar for stage use. It gives me plenty of time to trigger the next clip or scene; a bar is a long time!
- My songs are quite structured, but I always throw a few extra loops and one-shots into the set, usually as transitions in-between songs. It's a good chance to try out new loops and sounds on stage before incorporating them into 'proper' songs.
- When you rehearse your set, set everything up as you will on stage – with all interfaces connected, and any ReWired applications that you

intend to use. These will put a drain on your computer, and you should find out how much of a drain before – not during – the performance.

• If you've been tweaking your latency/buffer settings in Live's preferences, you may need to change these settings for performance use.

Song header scenes

Read about song header scenes in 'Clips And Scenes...' – very useful when working with big sets on stage.

Onstage troubleshooting

Some quick 'look outs' for stage use:

• Using a hardware controller on stage adds another layer of things to do. Take the M-Audio Ozonic as an example; you need to set this one up extra carefully – your audio's coming out of it too! The Ozonic is FireWire-based, and must be connected while the computer is off. Once the computer restarts, launch Live, and make sure the Ozonic is identified correctly; if necessary go to Audio and MIDI preferences, and select the Ozonic as the output/input source. Make sure you have the correct preset loaded on the Ozonic. Make sure the Ozonic's volume controllers are at the appropriate starting positions, and you've connected all necessary inputs/outputs at the back of the keyboard. Whatever device you use, you'll have to get into some sort of routine like this – that's one reason why I don't like to change my setup too often.

• Remember to connect your audio interface (a friend-who-shall-be-nameless forgot this at Cargo recently – long silence at the beginning of his set).

• Do you want to tweak your audio interface's knobs during the set? Don't put it on the floor, then.

• Getting interference? Try running your laptop from the battery instead of mains power.

• Remember to select your interface as input/output in Live's preferences.

• Go easy on hungry plug-ins. Maybe you should pre-render instruments and effects before the gig.

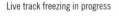

Live track freezing in progress

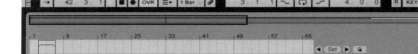

- Don't freeze or unfreeze tracks during your set – freezing will stop all audio, and unfreezing can produce pops or clicks.
- Oops! The Sudden Silence Syndrome: have you soloed a track? Have you got a filter or gate at an extreme setting?
- Most important, remember to have fun. You're quite safe with Live – it's very stable. What's the worst that could happen? Enjoy it…

Solo performance – J-Lab

J-Lab is one of the UK's most experienced Live performers; performing regularly at assorted clubs and dives around London. I've seen him jam with other laptop musicians, and perform Live solo sets. Here he shares some thoughts on solo performance with Live:

Quote

'I use Live 100% in live situations, about 75% in the studio. Most of my writing comes from a performance/improvisation angle, and since Live gained MIDI and VST/AU support, it's made Logic redundant for writing – though I still use it for mixing and mastering. Alongside Live I use Reason, radiaL, Pluggo, FM7, Pro53, Absynth, and PSP's Vintage Warmer. For hardware control I use a Novation Remote 25 and Motu 828 FireWire audio interface. No more mouse! Most of the sounds I use are recorded and composed by me. Any third-party samples get manipulated in some way – years of programming an E-MU 64 and fear of litigation turned me into a compulsive sample mangler! ' – J-Lab

J-Lab's Live set

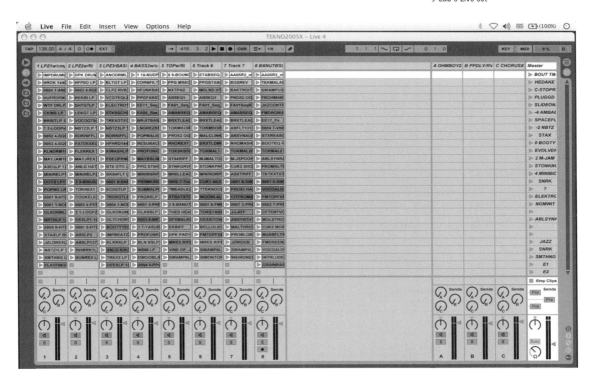

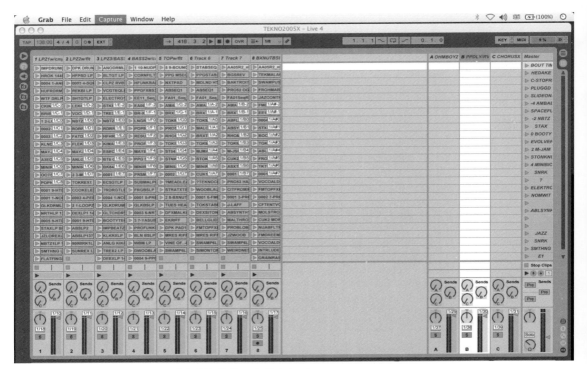

(Above) J-Lab's Live set with MIDI
assignments

(Below) J-Lab's Live set with keyboard
assignments

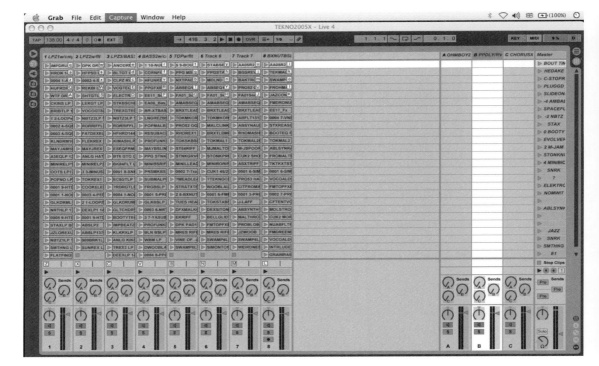

Generally I run 8 tracks live – my old G3 couldn't cope with more. For my techno stuff, the tracks are laid out like this:

1   Hard beats (with compressor)
2   Softer beats (with a filter)
3   Percussive/abstract rhythm (with a gate)
4   Bass (with a filter and compressor)
5   Lead (with a filter)
6   Secondary lead/harmony
7   Secondary lead/harmony
8   Weirdness and soundbites

I use three auxs – a mega 'performance' delay, a normal delay sharing with the Ableton Reverb, and whatever I feel like on the third aux. This setup has allowed me to accommodate most of the functionality on to the controller keyboard and get away from the laptop in the gig. All my clips are from tracks I've written or bits I'm messing with. There's no pre-arrangement, I just fire off whatever, and take it from there. No two gigs are ever the same, and normally something completely new comes out of them. To make it more interesting I quantize to an eighth note, so I can create new rhythmic possibilities.'

Info

You can use MIDI notes to select Live's tracks – used in conjunction with the scene scroll and select functions (also assignable) this gives you a way to navigate around tracks, scenes, and clips without touching the computer keyboard.

Jamming

See Chapter 15 'Using Live 5 with audio and MIDI interfaces' for a brief suggestion about setting up two laptops to jam together.

Using Live within a band – Songcarver/Keith Lang

Australian Keith Lang is another experienced Live performer, using it in his own solo sets as Songcarver, as well as in a band capacity. Keith is co-creator of Musolomo, a real-time VST performance sampler, which works within Live:

Quote

I use Live to trigger loops and play keyboard parts, and to process live guitar as part of a 5-piece pop/dance/funk band called Cocoa Jackson Lane. Generally the plug-ins I use are Musolomo – of course – and the MDA combo guitar distortion; sometimes a few others, all freebies. In the studio I also use the Logic instruments which were part of Logic 6. I use a Novation Remote25 MIDI controller, and a Motu 828 FireWire audio interface, alongside a few custom items.

I never use pre-made loops – all my sounds are from instruments or highly-edited 'natural' recordings – like me banging on pots and pans in the kitchen. I put all the songs in a single set, and my Novation has a bunch of 'sets' in it, which means the MIDI output changes for each 'set' I choose on my MIDI controller; Live just sits there and listens.

I usually group the loop-based stuff into five 'sections'. It's all triggered with no quantization and I have a cool custom setup for tempo which allows me to use some buttons for push/ pull and increase and decrease tempo by 2.5 bpm. There are times in the band context when I'm conscious of some of Live's shortcomings: time signature changes suck, and tempo changes are pretty blocky. It's very much a 4/4, block of 8 bars sort of thinking – the culture of dance music. It doesn't encourage a sense of harmonic progression. – *Keith Lang*

Session freeze in progress

Freezing tracks in the Session View

You can freeze tracks in the Session View, as well as the Arrangement View – the frozen track will be highlighted; see the screen shot. Clips will still launch and the mixer controls will still function, but you can't go into the clip to change anything. Perhaps you could use track freeze like this if you've got a software instrument track in your Live set and you don't want to bother

'Frozen' Session tracks playing

bouncing all the clips down to audio files.

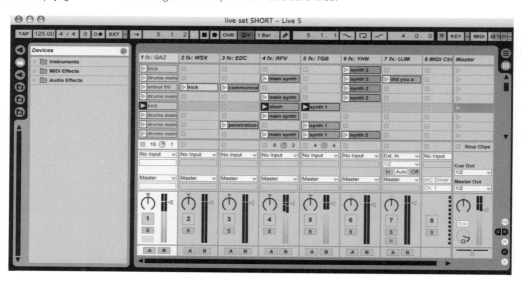

Jamming in the Arrangement View is just wrong

Because Live is so real-time oriented, it's possible to do a lot of jamming-type actions in the Arrangement View. The first time I saw Ergo Phizmiz do this, I must admit I was surprised, but there's always some crossover between Live's Views, and I guess this is a reflection of that. Certainly you can drag

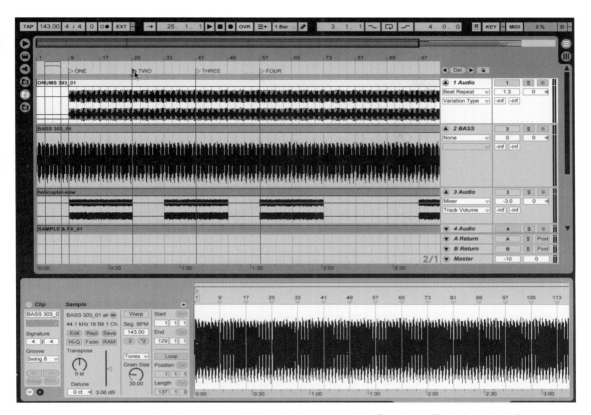

and drop your way around the Arrangement View, but in general the Session View is the place to improvise; although Live 5's new locators will only serve to encourage this kind of behaviour – allowing quantized movement between song sections, and real-time restructuring in the Arrangement View...hey, that sounds interesting...now they've got me at it...

Showing locators in the Arrangement View

Live in the theatre

Live has also found a place in theatres, where it's real-time operation means that music and sound effects can be delivered on cue, even if the cue does- n't quite come where it should! I had a quick word with Joe Young, who knows more about this sort of thing than I do:

Info

You can't record locator jumps as part of the automation in the Arrangement View.

Quote

I use Live only in performance – I use ProTools and radiaL for studio work. My hardware setup is a Pro Tools MBox and M-Audio Ozone controller keyboard. I use my own environmental sound recordings, plus samples from various sources – CD, vinyl, etc. I limit myself to 8 tracks of audio, so that I have enough hardware control on the Ozone. I have a rough score already worked out from rehearsals, and then I intuitively feed the sounds in during performance; I appreciate the ability to have a large number of pre- loaded sounds mapped and ready for performance. I see Live as a very sophisticated playback and processing machine, rather than an instrument. – *Joe Young*

VJing – video performance alongside Live

See Chapter 13 'Using Live 5 with other Software and Hardware' for information about using Live 5 with the popular Arkaos VJ software.

Info – shopping

If you're going on stage with Live, get a gooseneck-style USB light – it's probably the most useful piece of hardware you'll ever buy. I also like the MicFlex from MacMice – not a 'serious' studio tool, but good for anybody who wants to talk or do some vocal processing on stage – Live 5 adds proper support for mono mic sources. Plug in the MicFlex, and it appears in Live's preferences as an Input Audio Device called C-Media USB Headphone set (1 In, 0 Out). Go to an audio track in Live and choose Ext. In, then '1' rather than the more usual '1/2', and arm the track to record.

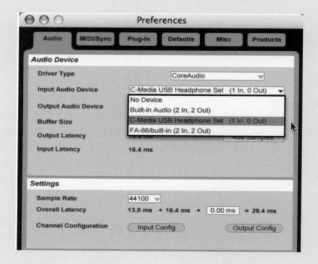

DJing with Live

Why is Live good for DJs?

I don't think it was planned that way, but Live is great for DJing. The DJs started to come on board early – some of the world's leading DJs are Live's most vocal supporters – and their input has influenced Live's development; we can all benefit from the new features that this has inspired. In fact, that's the reason why this section on DJing is so brief – everything in this book is relevant to DJing, just as it is to performance, or composition, or whatever else you're doing. See for example the section on mashups in 'Studio Notes'; see for example the section on the File Browser in 'Get Organised'...

Live's had DJ-friendly features for, well, forever, it seems: the way that entire songs (in AIF or WAV formats) can be browsed and dropped in as single clips, or cut into sections, and beat-matched by use of the warp markers; the pre-listening options; tap tempo; and of course the crossfader. Live 5 has emphasised this mutual DJ love-in with features like Auto-Warping, where songs (or long samples) are automatically issued with warp markers when they're imported; the new Complex warp mode, for material containing a mixture of beats and melodic parts; support for the inevitable MP3 file format; a Re-Pitch warp mode for more deck-like behaviour of audio clips; and nudge, where a looping clip's start point can be bumped backwards or forwards.

When DJs started using Live, they often tried to create a Live set which somehow related to their twin decks – based around a two-track system, with DJ-friendly plug-ins like EQ3 and Auto Filter; this has changed, as DJs have come to appreciate Live's power; the truth is, anything goes. I already mentioned the sections on mashups and the File Browser; you should also read about labelling clips and tracks in 'Clips And Scenes...', mapping and hardware controllers in 'Using Live 5 With Hardware Controllers', the Complex warp mode in 'Clips And Scenes...' and 'Live Talks To Itself!', building Live sets in 'Performance Notes', and the crossfader in 'Automation'.

Although it's not new to Live 5, Re-Pitch mode is worth a reminder. It's funny in a way – kind of undoing all that time-stretching technology; after going to all that trouble to stretch audio in a natural way, now we want it to change pitch with tempo again. Whether you're a DJ or not, Re-Pitch is a very useful creative effect, and sound mangling just wouldn't be the same without it (see Chapter 7 'Live Talks To Itself').

Info

PSP's Vintage Warmer is good for helping your laptop sit alongside decks, sonically speaking. It just gives everything a certain oomph; you will sound louder! Read more about Vintage Warmer in 'Devices'.

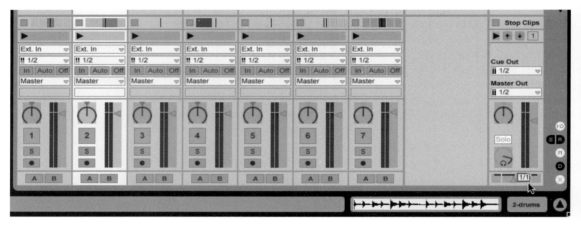

Live's cross fader

Cueing/Pre listening

If you've got an audio interface connected, like the M-Audio FW410, with at least 4 individual mono outputs, or 2 stereo pairs, you can configure it with Live for cueing (or pre-listening, as some people call it), like a DJ mixer. Audio in the Browser, and in selected tracks, can be monitored on, say, tracks 3+4, while the main mix goes to the PA on tracks 1+2. Use the Cue Out button to set this up – click on it, then choose Configure... which will open the Audio panel in Preferences. Then choose Channel Configuration/Output Config. Now you'll see a list of your hardware's outputs – make sure 1/2 (stereo) and 3/4 (stereo) are highlighted, then click OK, and close the windows. The knob below master track pan is your cue volume control, the button above that switches between solo mode and cue mode – when solo mode is engaged, the solo switches work as usual across the mixer, silencing all tracks other than those that are soloed. When cue mode is engaged, however, all output from the browser, and any soloed tracks can be pre listened on outputs 3 and 4.

Info

Mac OSX Tiger users can set-up for cueing even if their interface doesn't have the necessary facilities. See 'Using Live 5 With Audio and MIDI Interfaces'.

Info – Live clip cheats

Is it cheating to have an entire song on one Live clip, as some DJs do? No.

Live DJing with John 00 Fleming

'The main thing is that it completely reinvents the role of the DJ; we can perform live remixes and bootlegs on the dance floor; we can reconstruct any track the way we want it to happen, making our sets completely unique. Also, having your whole music collection with you on a tiny hard drive makes complete sense. Gone are the days of lugging around heavy record boxes; I don't understand DJs that still do this.

For hardware control I use the Evolution UC33, because it's like a mini mixing desk. The way I use Ableton (in performance) is how I work in the recording studio; to have as much control as possible is vital for me. There are many controllers around that are DJ based, they simply don't have enough control for me. I mix multiple tracks at the same time, loaded with effects!

I've just started using Echo Audio's Indigo DJ, because it's one less thing to plug in when you get to a gig. This simply slots into the laptop giving me 2 x stereo outputs. Seems to be perfect for the job in hand, I'm very pleased with it.

I use ReWire in the recording studio, but am not keen to use this in a club. The concept is a great one, but I've only just got to trust the new generation of laptops and operating systems, knowing that they wont crash on me. ReWire for me represents a disaster waiting to happen. When a crash happens in a club, it can seem to take forever to restart that computer...thankfully those days are over.'

The Indigo audio card

Studio notes

When I say 'studio', I'm basically talking about anything that isn't to do with performance; especially things which happen in the Arrangement View – songwriting, production, remixes, that kind of thing. As usual, refer to all other chapters in this book – the regular Live crossover warnings apply! These are just some brief random notes relating to 'the studio' that don't fit any-where else...

If you spend a lot of time in the Arrangement View, you'll be pleased by Live's new Locators; markers which allow you to jump around your song's timeline. There are little buttons for previous, set, and next locator. You can click anywhere in the timeline and create a locator. You can create locators while Live is playing. Even better, the locator set, previous, and next buttons

Track freeze/unfreeze via context menu

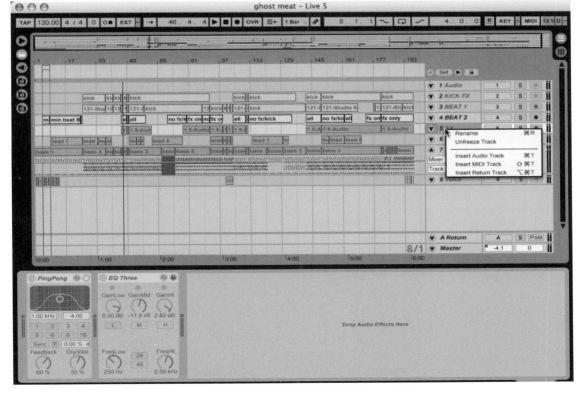

are MIDI and keyboard assignable, so you can use a MIDI controller to navigate the timeline. Ctrl-r/cmd-r on a locator to name it.

Track Freeze is another new Live 5 wrinkle – something that might be
familiar to users of other DAWs. It's used to cut the CPU load arising from
effects and software instruments. Select Freeze Track from the Edit menu, or
use the ever-present context menu, and a temporary audio reference file is
created for every clip in the track. Until the track is unfrozen, Live uses the
reference files instead of the devices in the track. This works very well – if
you're having any playback problems, or you're trying to run a Live set created on a more powerful computer, try it.

- Frozen plug-in tracks can be played on a computer that doesn't have the
  original plug-in.
- Mixer functions are still available for frozen tracks.

Track delay in Arrangement View

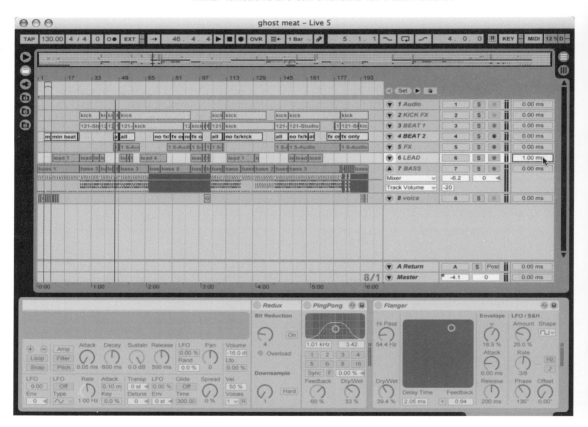

A new window in Live is a noteworthy addition: choose Track Delay from the
View menu (in either Arrangement or Session Views) and a small box appears
in the mixer section for each track in your set, displaying '0.00 ms'. Click and
drag in this field to introduce track delay. A higher value 'moves' the track
later (in comparison with the song), while a minus value will cause the track
to start playing earlier; values of plus/minus one second are possible.

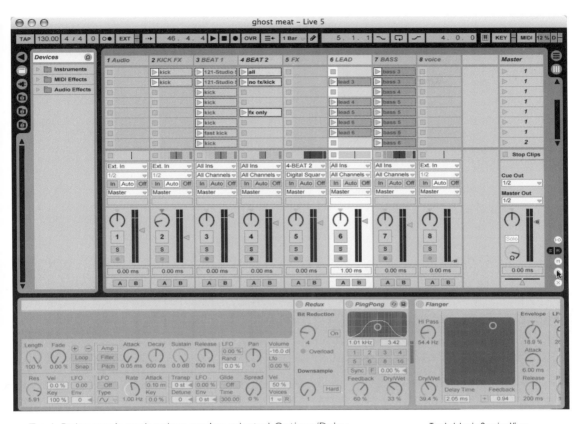

Track delay in Session View

- Track Delay won't work unless you've selected Options/Delay Compensation.

You may have noticed a new zone above the Arrangement View's track area – this is the Scrub Area. Click in here while your song's playing, and playback will jump to that point, according to your global quantization setting. If you click and hold, playback will loop, again, according to global quantization. If global quantization is off altogether, or very small, you can click and drag in the scrub area and hear your progress as you 'scrub' through – a term familiar to video editors.

- You can scrub in clips too (warping has to be on).
- You can't automate anything in the Scrub Area!
- See the ReWire coverage in 'Using Live 5 With Other Software & Hardware'.
- See 'Automation' for more Arrangement fun.

Songwriting
Live is a great tool for songwriting – although it may not look like it. With Live you can take a piece of music from the smallest germ of an idea to the finished overblown final production ('overblown' part optional). If you have a background of working with songwriting in a linear context, don't think you

have to abandon it all in favour of loop-based music; instead enjoy the opportunities available – you can combine the best of both worlds. I know some people who have had problems making the adjustment to songwriting in Live, but it really isn't that different, and it's much more intuitive to work with song structures in Live than in Logic, for example.

If you need a beat to work over, just drag something in from the Browser, or create a MIDI clip, drop in Impulse, and create your own drum part. While these beats are looping, start working with some MIDI clips – draw in, or input from a keyboard – then go through your sample library for other sounds that might fit. Record a live instrument or voice and throw that in the mix. The great thing with Live is that you don't have to stop playback, you can just keep building the layers, and, as you create more clips, you can start moving and copying them, trying out new structures while the clips are still playing.

When I'm writing songs in Live, there's always one sound that kicks it all off – even if I come to it with a melodic idea, it doesn't really start working until a certain sound appears, whatever it might be. Live has so many alleyways you can get lost in, but as you understand it better, it starts working for you – you're not just following the software anymore. If you've got any old songs that you put on ice because they weren't getting anywhere, throw them into Live and see what happens – it can help you see your songs from different perspectives; Live makes it easy to import existing parts, and of course to manipulate them freely – it can help you isolate the germ that made your song work in the first place, and put it in a different (hopefully better) setting. This re-use of old material crosses into the jamming/remix/mashup philosophies that Live embraces.

• Songs made in Live don't have to be loop-based, they don't have to be 'dance' music, they don't have to sound 'electronic'.

Info - toomuchchoiceitis

Live has a relatively simple interface, but it's still easy to lose your perspective - too much choice! If you're starting to feel blocked, give yourself some limitations to work against. For example I had a song I was struggling to finish, it had 8 or 9 tracks, with drums, percussion, various synths and basses. All the parts worked individually, but somehow they didn't hang together as a song. Rather than delete any parts or change the basic structure, I made a rule: only four tracks could be playing at any time, so the tracks would have to 'take turns'. It worked great - cleared the air a little bit. Cutting things down is nearly always a good idea - I'm quite ruthless when working on remixes; you start rooting around in a track and you find things that don't need to be there. Live's Arrangement View makes it a snap to do things like this, using a combination of actions such as splitting clips, and automation track activation/deactivation. Make your own rules - they could apply to effects, or the number of scenes or clips...whatever it takes.

Remixes and mashups with Live

Live is the ultimate remix/mashup tool. I've done them before with other DAW software, but Live takes away the torture involved in all that slicing and rearranging. There were times when certain decisions were based on wanting to get it over with, rather than what was going to sound good. Tempo manipulation used be the worst thing about remixing – it was time-consuming, and any changes to a song's original tempo were restricted to a narrow range.

(Opposite page)
A mashup in progress in Session View

A mashup in Arrangement View

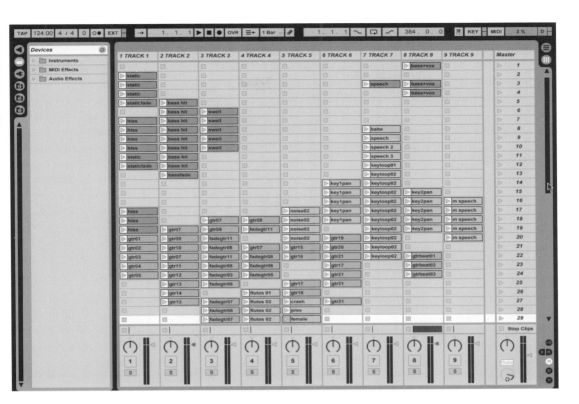

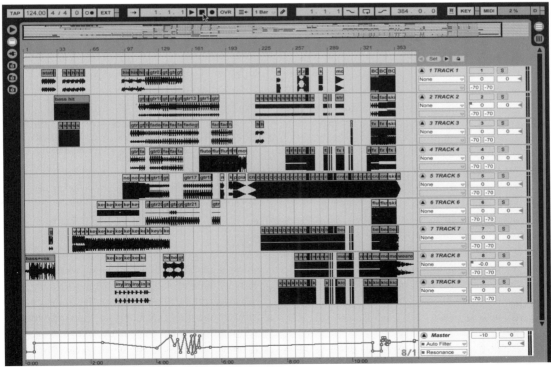

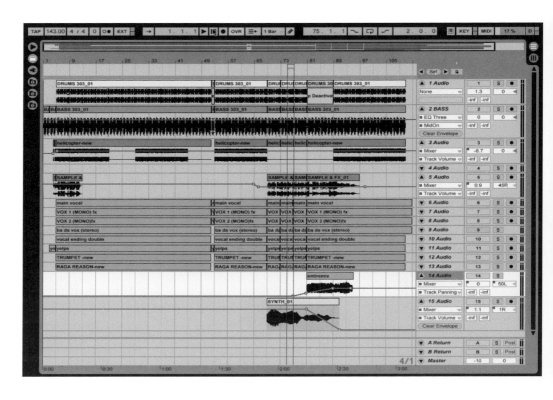

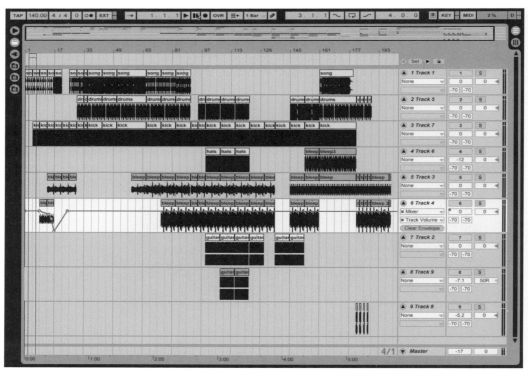

Live has made it almost invisible, and the new Auto-Warp feature is the icing on the cake. It's just too easy! It's cheating! Then once everything is locked into time, you can add as much other stuff as you want – how about more audio clips, or software instrument parts? Resample sections and re-process them; whatever gets the job done.

Remixing and mashups are where DJing and 'musicianship' meet – Live makes it so easy to drop parts of other people's songs into your own – or to drop your own sounds into other people's songs. For one mashup I did of two 1970s songs, I recorded myself singing and playing bass through the mic of my laptop, and used that in the intro. Throughout the song I added some speech from a TV documentary, and some other sounds that I recorded on minidisc a year or two earlier (in my live set, I have drums from 8-track cassette demos I made 15 years ago – and they sound great – hissy, but great).

These are the mashup baby steps:

*   Find two songs you want to work with. Live makes it easy to fit anything to almost anything else, but you still need to apply some good taste!

*   Load and Auto-Warp the songs to adjoining audio tracks (in the Session View). Although you can use MP3s, the finished mix will sound better if you use full quality AIFs or WAVs.

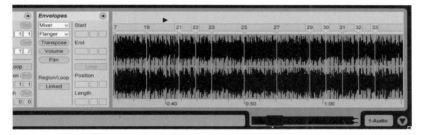

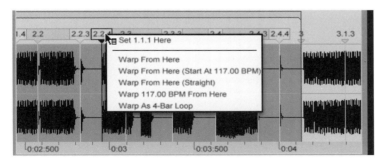

*   Check both songs have warped correctly; sometimes the intros need looking at.
*   Go through the songs and find the sections you want to use. Isolate the

(Opposite page)
Different mashups in Arrangement View

Showing auto warping in progress

Showing auto warping completed

Showing the auto warp context menu options

sections into separate clips. Define the start and end points of the sections (they're probably going to be loops).

- Remember that Live can zoom right in for finer cuts, if you want to make very small slices.
- Consolidate the clips, to trim away the junk (this will necessitate a quick detour to the Arrangement View).
- Choose the best-sounding warp modes for your clips – do this on an individual basis. Sometimes the 'right' warp mode isn't the 'best'.
- You might need to adjust the volumes of the various clips – I use the clip gain sliders for this, so it doesn't interfere with anything i might do at track level.
- Structure the mashup as you see fit. It can be clever, or groovy, or funny, or totally destructive – you are in control.
- When you're done, record it into the Arrangement View; if inspiration strikes during the recording process and it takes you off on a tangent – go with it.
- Mix the finished mashup to a stereo master, then hide from the authorities! Of course these projects should only be undertaken for your own entertainment. the laws of copyright are very strict :-)

Live is top dog at this – there's no competition.

Movie notes

Movie soundtracks with Live – it can be done

Using Live to score movies wasn't on the radar when it was launched. However, the superior 'time-management' features that make Live so useful for everything else, also make it ideal for fitting audio to movies. In this world of digital video, last-minute changes to edits are more common than ever, and you need a comparable way of working with audio...enter Live. Live doesn't have QuickTime movie support – not as I write this, anyway – so what makes it such a hot proposition that composers are willing to go to some inconvenience, finding workrounds to make it work?

Quote

'Whenever the director makes picture changes, I will not have to make cuts anymore, but simply stretch time. We change a lot of things in the final dub. This is when the sound effects come in, sometimes the whole feel of the movie changes. This always is a great moment. It is fantastic to be able to manipulate things, to make changes at the very last moment. There is this fine line between writing and manipulating. This is an ongoing process. So, rather than delivering things in Pro Tools and doing cuts all the time, Live makes things much easier.' - *Hans Zimmer*

It's ironic – Live is the best video soundtrack tool around that can't view video! Every major DAW has the ability to open QuickTime movies, and if Ableton want to compete, they'll have to add this feature; I'm sure it's on the way. In the meantime, there are movies to be soundtracked, and we don't want to use anything apart from Live to do them. There are some workrounds that'll let us use our favourite 'sequencing instrument'...

Live movie method 1 – ReWire Live to another DAW

This one isn't a 'cheat' or 'workround' – it's the regular way of doing it. Bite the bullet and ReWire Live to another DAW. Simple as that. Read more about ReWire in the chapter on 'Using Live 5 With Other Software & Hardware'.

Live movie method 2 – the 'fake' Live QuickTime window

If you want to give Live a dedicated QuickTime Player, you can fake it, again by ReWiring it to your DAW of choice. I'm using Logic as the example here, but any ReWire/QuickTime compatible DAW should give similar results.

Logic has to be the ReWire master, so you must launch it first, then create a new project. Import a QuickTime version of your movie, open Logic's movie window, and delete all unused tracks. Close all Logic windows apart from the movie window, and position it somewhere you can see it when Live is running. Open your Live set, and let ReWire do its magic – whenever you start/stop/scrub in Live, the movie will follow right along. Make sure you allocate a couple of Logic tracks to ReWire L and ReWire R, otherwise you won't hear anything from Live. If you're not running any other tracks or software instruments in Logic, this method shouldn't be too demanding of your computer. Maybe if you've got two computers you can run Live on one and Logic on the other, and sync them over a network. You could also use Live 5's new locators, enabling you to skip around different edit points in the movie. This isn't a perfect method by any means, but it works in a way – give it a try.

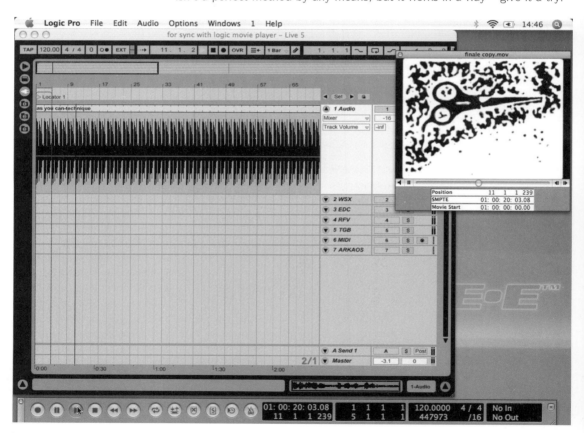

Live with Logic's movie window

Info – Live's useful movie tools

What's helpful when you're using Live for movie soundtracks:

Warping – stretch your audio or music to fit movie edits.
ReWire – synchronize Live to a movie-friendly DAW, like Logic or Cubase, or to the ReVision QuickTime player.
Locators – use Live 5's new locators to label and jump between key movie edit points.

Live movie method 3 – the ReVision player

Granted Software's ReVision is a ReWire-compatible QuickTime player that plays QuickTime movies and syncs via ReWire to applications such as Live and Reason. Before I continue – ReVision is Mac-only!

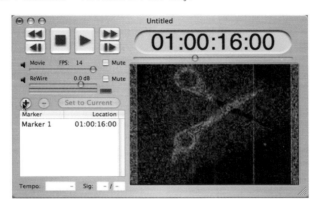

The ReVision player

Live with ReVision player's markers

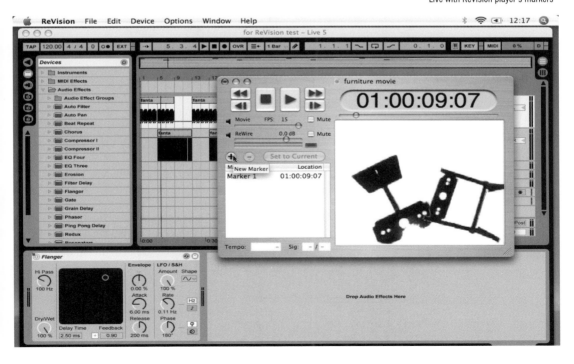

Showing ReVision's renamed markers

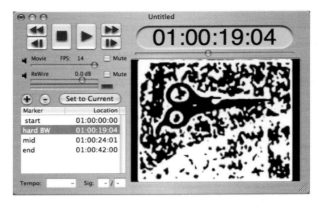

ReVision allows the creation of markers (with tempo and time signature changes for each if required), standalone movie play (so you can insert markers into a movie before opening Live), scrubbing, movable timecode origin, movie start offset, and the option to export the QuickTime movie complete with new audio track.

The ReVision export window

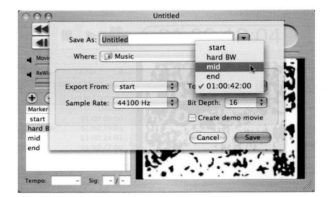

Here's a quick run-down of how it works. Launch ReVision first (ReWire master, remember?), then import your QuickTime movie into it. Don't waste system resources with a large, high quality version of the movie – render a cheap'n'cheerful one for this job. You can go through the movie and add markers immediately, if you want to; hit the spacebar to play, then click on the '+' button to add markers. Once you've finished entering your markers, you can go back and name them; you can also 'nudge' their positions using your computer's left'/right arrows and the 'set to current' button. You can scrub in ReVision, so if you prefer, you can just hop straight to specific points and drop in the markers. Once you've got your markers organised, open Live. There's a shortcut to open Live in ReVision's 'Device' menu, but it doesn't work, so you'll have to do it manually (ReVision searches for all ReWire slave-compatible apps on your computer, and you can sync from ReVision to several apps at once).

From then on, Live will work in it's usual ReWire slave mode – the native effects and instruments are available, third-party ones are not. This needn't be a big problem – once you've got your basic soundtrack mapped out, you could work with the plug-ins later, running Live on its own. Of course, Live has its own markers now, the locators in the Arrangement View, but I couldn't persuade ReVision to work with them properly – best to let ReVision give the orders! Use the volume sliders in ReVision to mute or balance the audio from the QuickTime movie and from Live.

Once you've finished your soundtrack (see how I skipped over that difficult 'creative' part?), you're ready to export the finished project. You can export the audio from ReVision's File menu, and you'll get an option to include a reference movie as well. If you want to play with some third-party plug-ins in Live now, quit Live, quit ReVision, then relaunch Live and all of your AU's and VSTs will be back on board.

Mac with two displays

Frank Blum is one of a growing number of composers who have found the ReVision/Live combo (almost) ideal for making music to fit a movie:

Quote

'I´m working on a soundtrack for a 90-minute TV movie, for this I compose all music with Live 5. There's only one possibility for bringing QuickTime movies into Live at the moment – connect Live via ReWire with ReVision. The bad thing is it only works with ReVision as ReWire master and Live as ReWire slave; that means no VST-plug-ins, and I normally use them a lot. So what I do is first work with Simpler, Operator, Impulse and the other Live internal effects to get the sync points. Luckily now Live 5 has locators, which helps a lot to mark significant frames in the movie. Then later I change some instruments, for example, replace an Operator sound with a Reaktor synth, resample it (so it´s an audio file) and start it again with ReVision to check it and so on. It´s a bit complicated but this work-around for composing with Live instead of Cubase or other apps which can view QuickTime movies makes it much easier for me to do what I want.'
– *Frank Blum*

Info

ReVision and Live battle for screen space on smaller displays, like laptops; as always when ReWiring, things go better if you use a second display. ReVision can 'float' above Live, even if you're running Live in full screen mode.

Teaching notes

How to get somebody hooked on Live

If you want to get somebody hooked on Live, this is what to do (they'll thank you for it later):

1 Create an empty Live set, with five audio tracks. Work in the Session View. Set global quantization to 1 Bar.
2 Put one audio effect on each track ('fun' things like delays, not 'sensible' things like EQ), and an Auto Filter on the master track.
3 Drag'n'drop four audio clips into each track, and make sure they're nice bright colours.
4 The majority of clips should be set to loop, but include a couple of one-shots.
5 Enter Key Map Mode (Ctrl-k/cmd-k), and assign a letter of the alphabet to every clip. Label each clip with the letter that triggers it.
6 Set the launch mode of all clips to 'Toggle' in the Launch box (or set 'toggle' as the default in Preferences/Defaults).
7 Choose a one-shot – preferably a speech sample – and quantize it to 1/16ths, change its launch mode to Trigger, and disable looping.
8 Use Key Map Mode to assign letters to the effect on/off buttons.
9 Name each track with the letter necessary to fire that track's effect.
10 Hide the browser, in/outs, overview, sends, etc – clear the decks, and enter full screen mode (see the screen shot overleaf for a view of the overall set).

The key mapping allows beginners to get a groove going in the shortest possible time, and with the minimum of explanation. You can tell your students to just start pressing letters and observe what happens. Toggle Mode means you don't have to explain how to start/stop individual tracks, all they need is the spacebar to start/stop the entire set. With the one-bar global quantization, clips always come in on time, and the 1/16th quantization for selected one-shots adds that extra 'DJ scratching a record' vibe – tacky though it is, newcomers love that kind of thing, especially kids. I've used a set based on this format to introduce Live to all kinds of people – it creates a game-like environment, emphasising the fun and real-time control that Live offers. The next step is to explain more about the effects, the mixer (mainly why red level meters are a Bad Thing), tempo changes, and recording what they're doing; then viewing and editing it all in the Arrangement view.

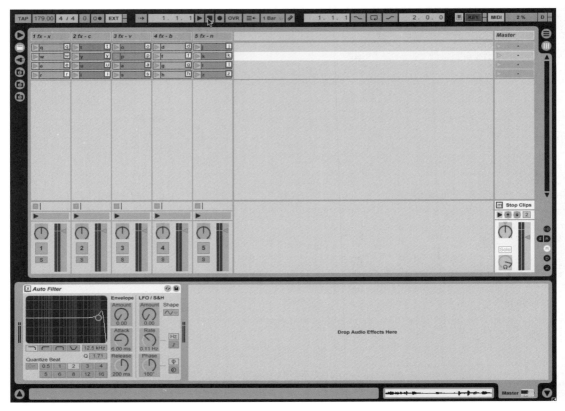

Keyboard mapping

Finally, add some transposition to the 1/16th clip – as your student constantly re-triggers the speech sample, get them to move the clip's Transpose knob up and down, they'll love it.

In the classroom with Live

I've taught Live to 'regular' school kids, kids with attention problems, adults with learning difficulties, prisoners, people in drug rehab, youth centres, students at risk of dropping out of college, and patients in secure psychiatric units. Live can seem complicated, but it's really down to how you introduce it to the students; taking time to set up a good Live demo file will make all the difference. Remember to take advantage of Live's ability to hide interface elements, so you can focus the students' attention where you want it. Even on one-day courses, I've had kids jamming with clips and effects, recording their voices, then recording it and editing automation. The real-time control wins them over, especially once they start recording their own sounds. Kids love that old-school sampling stuff like recording a beat being banged out on a plastic chair, and using warp markers to lock it to a tight rhythm. Nothing beats GarageBand for drag'n'drop simplicity, if you want to show people how to build songs in a linear fashion, but Live has the advantage of the real-time performance elements as an attention-grabber, and then of course it goes on from there, to far deeper levels of creativity. This is also where Ableton's one-product philosophy pays off – people love to know that the friendly, colour-

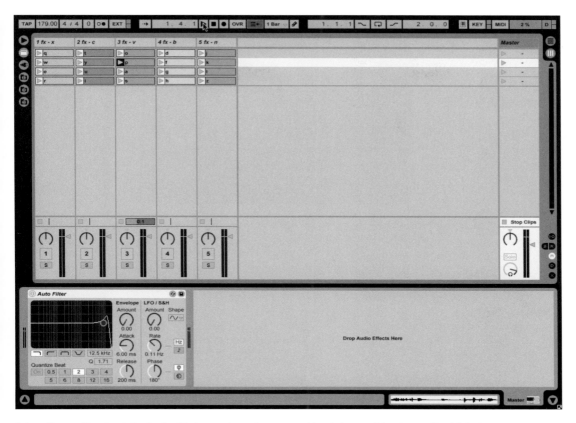

Completed set

ful, software they're 'playing' with is used on stages, and in clubs, and in studios, and in movies, around the world. You might not think of yourself as a
'teacher', but with the right combination of Live knowledge, general musical
experience, personality...you could have a lot to offer...and it's a two way
thing; you learn a lot too.

I did a project recently where we had groups of kids in four-day blocks.
The kids worked in pairs, spending the first two days creating a song in Live,
and the second two days remixing it. This gave us a chance to do things like
working with tempo changes, and bouncing down 4-bar chunks of the original mix to a single track, then looping and mangling it. They also experi-
mented with envelopes – drawing curves in empty tracks, and then pasting
them onto parameters in other tracks (volume, tempo, effects levels, cut-off,
etc), and listening to the quite random results. Quite 'conceptual', but also
fun – and some great sounds came from it.

During another recent project, one of the 11-year olds mentioned that he
could play guitar. I showed him a demo movie from the Ableton site about
working with guitars, and we had him recording guitar loops, working with
plug-ins, transposing down to create bass parts, and sharing the sounds with
his fellow students: his first experience of recording guitars. It was a fantastic time in the class, with the other kids making suggestions about what he
could play for them, and he was – of course – very excited and proud to be
'used' in this way.

An 11-year old girl jamming with Live

Working in classrooms with Live will teach you more about it too, especially when you hear some of the great stuff that kids will come up with. It reminds you that there's a lot of BS around electronic music – you start to realise how much of what you hear is really the software talking; how easy it is to be average with this kind of music, and how hard it is to be really good!

Using Live 5 with other software and hardware

In general, I favour using Live on its own – bouncing its ever-expanding feature set against its limitations; however, the real world is full of reasons for Live to communicate with other music gear – maybe one application does something another doesn't, or maybe you've got a song created in Logic, and you need it to run alongside Live. On the hardware side, you may want to set Live at the heart of your studio, triggering sounds and effects on hardware synths or samplers, or syncing via MIDI Clock or MIDI Timecode to hardware recording systems. And then you may enter other realms; controlling VJ equipment, lighting rigs – anything that can be controlled with MIDI.

ReWire

ReWire was created by Propellerhead, makers of Reason, to synchronise music applications; it's become standard – all sequencers now include ReWire support. It's invisible – you don't have to buy it, or install it separately – you hardly even have to tell it to do anything. The level of integration between ReWired applications varies, from basic sync, to streaming MIDI and audio through each other's inputs/outputs. In any ReWire setup, one application takes the role of Master, the other (or others) Slave(s). These roles are dictated by a simple means – the application that's opened first is the master. Some apps play both roles equally well, others insist on being boss.

Live and Reason – somebody has to be in charge

Reason is Propellerhead's incredibly popular software studio – the one that looks like a hardware rack. Reason doesn't cut it as a standalone production centre: the interface is inefficient, and Live has superior audio facilities; Reason can't record audio – it's purely a synth and sampling system (and a sampler without recording is...well...). ReWire brings these two together, allowing you to enjoy the best of each.

ReWiring Live with Reason is easy. Launch Live first, then Reason, to establish the ReWire relationship. In Reason, create some instruments and program some parts for each. Hit the spacebar to start/stop play in either the Reason or Live window, they'll play in sync. You won't hear anything though, until you route Reason through Live's outputs. In your first available Live audio track, choose 'Reason' from the Input menu. The Input Channel slot below that should display '1/2, mix L/R', representing Reason's main stereo output. If both apps are playing, you'll see some activity on the small meter

Showing typical Reason rack

in the Input channel slot. You STILL won't hear anything until you arm that Live track by clicking on the 'arm' button – it'll turn red. Now you've got Reason coming through, you can process it and record it into audio clips like anything else coming through Live.

Render without recording

It's possible to render Reason parts from Live without recording them first. Let's say you want to render 8 bars of Reason parts as part of your Live song. In the Arrangement View, click and drag to highlight the first 8 bars of the Live timeline, even though there's nothing to represent the Reason parts. Hit shift/command/r to render. Anything in your Live set is rendered, as well as the first 8 bars of your Reason song. This works even if you have no audio or MIDI content at all in Live, and are just looking at an empty Arrangement View. You can use this method to render your Reason material through Live-

Reason outputs in Live

hosted plug-ins – you can do fun stuff by drawing in automation for effects and mixer parameters in the empty Live audio track, and then rendering the Reason output through it.

Live set sending automation to Reason

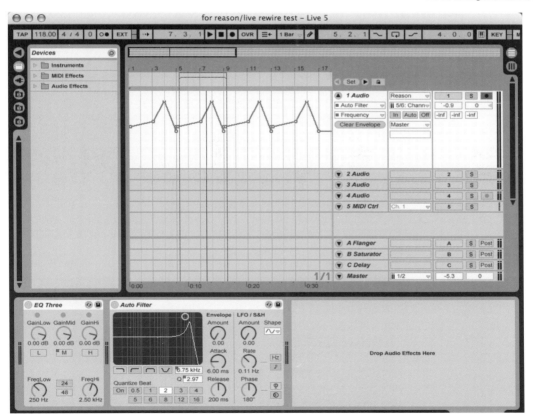

However, you'll probably want individual Reason instruments to go to separate Live tracks – click on the Reason '1/2, L/R' in the Input slot, to see a list of available Reason outputs. None of them will do anything yet, because at the moment all Reason parts are coming from the main stereo output. So, back to the Reason rack...hit 'tab' to flip the rack over. At the top, you'll see the back of the hardware interface – the only component that can't be removed from a Reason rack (by the way, when ReWire has been invoked, the front of the hardware interface says 'rewire slave mode').

Rear view of Reason
hardware interface

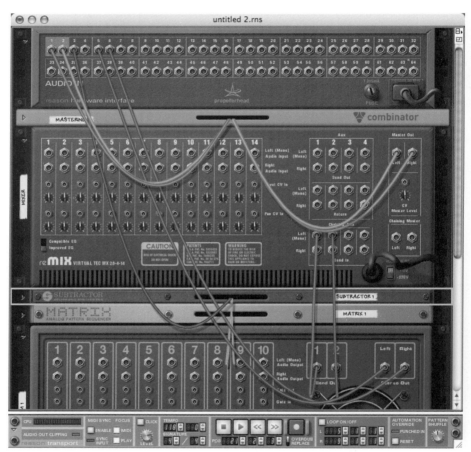

You'll notice that your mixer's left/right master outs are going to inputs 1/2 in the hardware interface – the main stereo out. Go to each Reason device, and drag its main output cables, whether mono or stereo, to separate inputs in the hardware interface. Let's say Redrum is going to 3/4, for example. Now, when you go back to Live, create a second audio track, and for that one choose 3/4, instead of 1/2. Arm it, start playing, and you'll hear your drum track coming through separately from the rest of the Reason mix. Mute track 1 to check it! Repeat this procedure for remaining Reason parts. This gives you the ability to mix, process and record the Reason parts separately within Live. You can delete the mixer altogether if you don't think you'll need it.

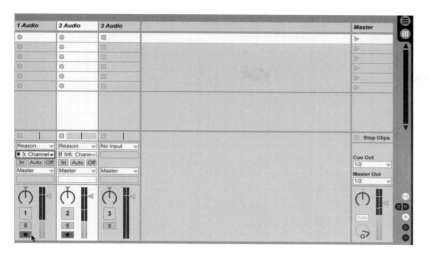

Showing individual Reason outputs in Live

Although it's great to be able to render a Live/Reason song without having to record the Reason material as audio first, it's still a good idea to create AIF or WAV versions of anything you create with MIDI. Over time, your setup changes, software is updated, obsoleted...things happen, and you're unable to use that original software instrument or preset; you can't recreate the sound in your song (note that safety on a computer is a relative concept).

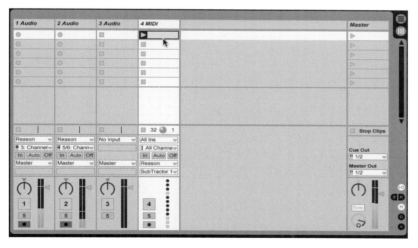

Showing MIDI sent from Live to Reason, and audio received from Reason

Reason won't send MIDI to Live, but it works fine the other way round. Create a MIDI track in Live, and choose Reason as it's Output Type. In the output chooser slot below that, you'll see a list of every device in your Reason rack. Choose one, then you can send MIDI notes and controllers to Reason. Of course, you can be sending MIDI to Reason at the same time as dealing with it's incoming audio on adjoining tracks.

When you've finished working with any ReWire combination, remember to quit the slave first. Well, even if you forget, it's pretty easy – Live will just refuse to go until Reason is quit first!

What's the catch?

There's a price to pay when running Live as a ReWire slave. Although the Live Device plug-ins will continue to work as usual, click on the Plug-In Device Browser for third-party plug-ins and you'll be greeted by this message: 'Unfortunately, plug-ins are deactivated when running Live as a ReWire slave.' If the Live set that you're opening already contains third-party plug-ins, you'll see the following message: 'failed to open audio unit (or VST) "NAME OF PLUG IN". audio unit could not be opened.

You'll also find that Live can't access any audio ins/outs – in Audio Preferences you'll see a message saying 'Live is running in ReWire slave mode. Audio I/O is handled by the ReWire master application. Sample rate 44100 (or whatever)'.

ReWiring Live to other sequencers

Logic is our example here, because it's what I use – the principles are similar with other sequencers like Cubase, though. Launch Logic first, then Live. The Live start-up window will display the following message: 'running as rewire slave'. let's say you have 3 Live audio tracks. Load a clip in each track and start them playing. In the Output slot for the first audio track, choose ReWire Out, and in the lower slot choose bus 3 (1 & 2 are for stereo output). For your second audio track repeat the procedure, choosing bus 4, and for the third track, 5. In Logic create 3 audio tracks. for Logic track 1 choose ReWire:

Logic's Arrange view

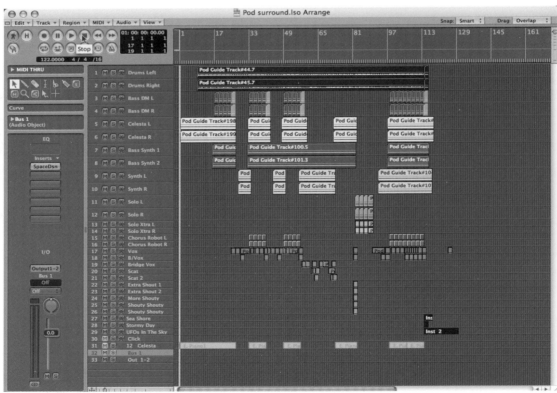

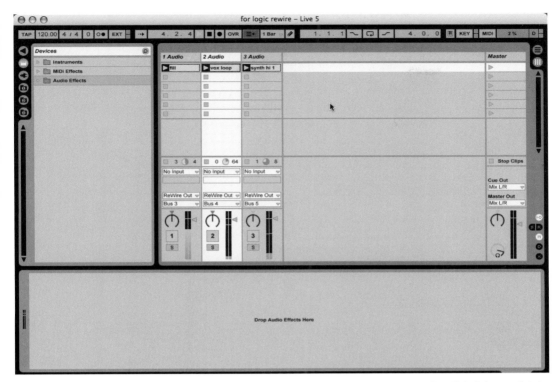

RW Bus 3 from the channel pop-up, and repeat for the other tracks choosing Bus 4-5. This is just an example – you can also choose pairs of ReWire outputs, like Bus 3.4. You don't have to arm the Logic tracks for recording; as soon as you start a clip playing on each Live track, their output will be audible through Logic – you'll see the input levels in the meter for each track. You can then record the Live inputs, and/or apply Logic's effects. If you have a MIDI controller routed to your Live MIDI track, you should also be able to hear the output from that when you hit the controller's pads or keys.

Down another Mac-only alley – ReWiring Live to GarageBand

You can ReWire Live to GarageBand; the question isn't 'how?', but 'why?'. It's a sync-only thing, with GarageBand as master; there's no way to route audio between them, but when you render your GarageBand mix, your Live parts are included. No set-up necessary, just launch GarageBand, then launch Live.

If you consider that GarageBand songs are Logic-compatible, then maybe there's something in it; you could create a quick GarageBand/Live project, then move the GarageBand portion to Logic for more 'professional' attention, and an open flow of audio and MIDI between the two. Yeah, that must be it!

There's a free Audio Unit called MidiO, which allows GarageBand to send MIDI to other applications. This works alongside ReWire to add another dimension to our unholy union. Launch GarageBand, then Live. Create a software instrument track in GarageBand, and click on the icon for the instrument. A window opens where you can select MIDI Out as the generator. Click the

Live with Logic busses selected

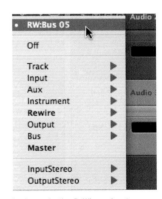

Logic – selecting ReWire as input source

GarageBand 'export to iTunes' mixing option

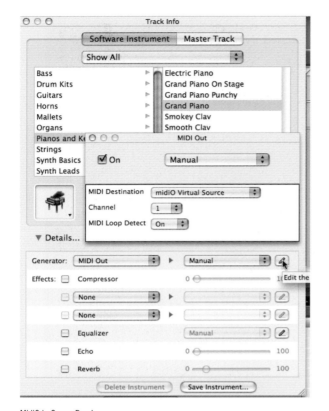

MidiO in GarageBand

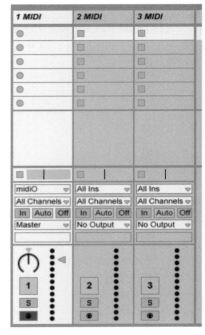

MidiO input in Live

'details' triangle if this option isn't showing, it's in the lower portion of the window. Click on the pencil box on the right to open another small window. Choose 'MIDI loop detect' ON and close the window. Record some notes, or import a software instrument Apple Loop. Deselect the GarageBand track to avoid creating a MIDI loop.

Now go to Live, create a MIDI track, and load Operator. Select a groovy preset. From the track's input slot, choose MIDI Out, then arm the track. Start GarageBand, and you should hear Operator playing the notes from GarageBand. You could use this to record GarageBand MIDI parts into Live, or to record audio from the GarageBand MIDI part by routing the output from the Live MIDI track to another Live audio track and recording it. Perverse as this seems, you can bet there's somebody out there doing it!

Arkaos VJ

VJing is the art of creating real-time video mixes in venues where bands or DJs are at play, and Arkaos VJ is one of the best VJ applications around. It's cross-platform, MIDI and ReWire friendly, and works great with Live; you can play a Live set and run synced visuals from your computer at the same time. Obviously, state-of-the-art computers are preferred for this, but with care you can do it on more humble systems – don't run too many tracks or plug-ins in Live, and keep your movie sizes down. Download the Arkaos VJ demo and try it. Here's how it works...

General view of Arkaos interface

Let's assume you have a LIve set ready to go, with audio or MIDI clips in the Session View. Create a new MIDI track, and name it 'Arkaos'. Launch Arkaos. Select Arkaos as an output destination in the slot at the bottom of the Live MIDI track. Live communicates with Arkaos via ReWire; it'll send MIDI only – there's no way to send audio to Arkaos. Now create MIDI clips as usual, sending notes to Arkaos as if it was a software instrument within Live; the only difference is that these notes trigger images, not sounds. You can even use Live's clip automation to send MIDI controllers to Arkaos' effects. Arkaos VJ doesn't have MIDI learn, so you'll have to enter controller numbers for each parameter; a slow process if you're using a lot of images, but the results are worth it – close integration between your music and visuals.

Arkaos as ReWire destination in Live

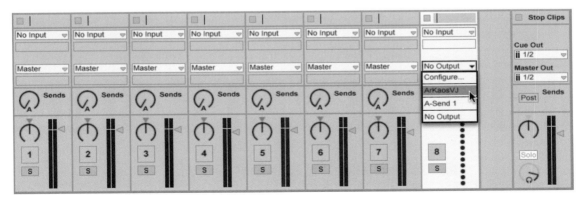

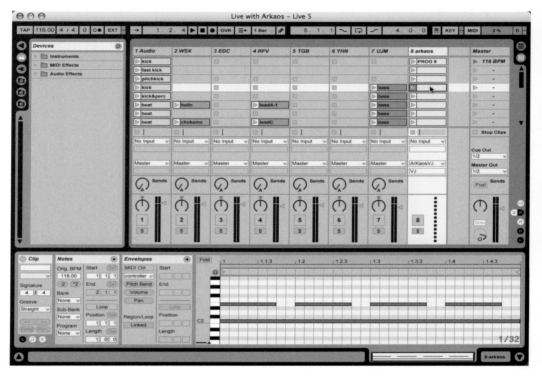

MIDI notes being sent from Live to
Arkaos

Arkaos with 'virtual keyboard'

Click on the MIDI keyboard at the bottom left of the Arkaos patch window to
see the 'virtual keyboard' that corresponds to the vertical 'piano roll' keyboard in Live's MIDI Note Editor. Drag'n'drop your images in position, draw

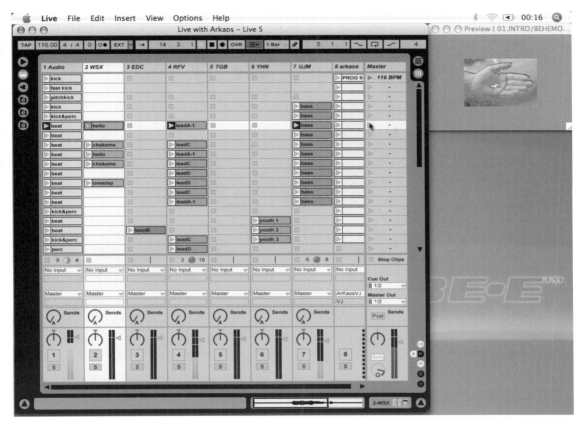

in the appropriate notes in Live, and hit play; Arkaos will begin to do its thing. Experimentation is rewarded: different note lengths will cause movies to play for more or less of their entirety. A Live MIDI clip can send a program change – the Program Change Select box is in the 'Notes' box in the Clip View – and you can use these to load the next Arkaos patch; I use a separate patch for each song. Rename the MIDI clips in the Live 'Arkaos' track to help you identify them quickly. There's no reason why you can't run Live in full screen and obscure Arkaos completely, it'll still feed your video projector as long as you've got display mirroring turned off. However, I like to close all other Arkaos windows, shrink the preview window down small, then stick it in the top right of my screen. I drag Live's window out as large as possible, without entering full screen or obscuring the Arkaos preview.

It's fascinating to compose with music and video at the same time. After a while the boundaries disappear, and you become a true A/V superstar!

Live and Arkaos together for performance use

Info

See Chapter 11 'Movie Notes' to read about ReWiring Live to ReVision, for movie soundtrack work.

MIDI Time Code and MIDI Clock

Live can send or receive MIDI Time Code (MTC) and MIDI clock. Very useful for communicating with MIDI-compatible hardware devices, such as sequencers, synths, samplers, grooveboxes, and lighting systems. Using Live with an external hardware device, such as a synth or sampler or sound module, is pretty much like ReWiring it to other software. Most of your setup time will be spent rooting around in the manual for the hardware in question; as usual there are few complications to deal with at the Live end. A common cause of problems is channel numbers – make sure both devices are on the same channel, ie 1, or choose 'omni' mode, which means the devices will look for MIDI on all channels. Live's MIDI clips can send MIDI controllers (CCs), bank changes, or program changes, so you can send MIDI to other applications and hardware with exactly the regular Live freedom.

Live's ability to send MIDI can come in handy even in simple situations, for example I use it to send MIDI Clock to a Boss GT-6B bass effects processor, to keep the bass delay effects in sync with my Live set. I've also sent MIDI to the GT-6B via an M-Audio FW410, and an Edirol FA-66 without any problems. Just watch those channel numbers!

GT-6B effects unit

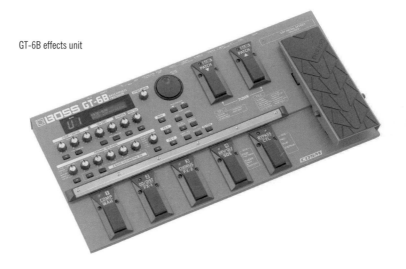

Using Live 5 with hardware controllers

A hardware controller is a device with a keyboard, and/or knobs and faders, that sends MIDI messages to your music software. Pretty much any MIDI hardware controller that's designed to work with a computer these days will have a USB connection, which is good because it's simple, like plugging in a printer, and the controller can draw power from the computer instead of using a dedicated power supply. Some controllers double as audio interfaces – containing necessary sockets for microphones and instruments; these often connect via FireWire or USB2 rather than regular USB. With Live, MIDI messages can be used to control track volume and panning, effects levels, transport , clip/scene/track selection, and – of course – to trigger actual musical notes or samples.

Info – best of both worlds

There's no substitute for going on stage with a Live-equipped laptop and a MIDI hardware controller. And there's no substitute for going on stage with a Live-equipped laptop and nothing else. A contradiction? Both are valid, and it's interesting to vary your approach occasionally.

Everybody who uses Live dabbles with hardware controllers at some time; it's common to end up with a collection of the things. Let's have a look at a selection of hardware – some keyboards, some controllers, some with audio interfaces – and see what each brings to its partnership with Live.

M-Audio Oxygen8

Long in the tooth as these things go, but still a good match for Live, the Oxygen8 has 25 keys and 8 knobs, with 5 presets. It can be powered from USB, mains power, or batteries. I've used the keyboard to trigger Live's scenes – up to 25 in the first song, then a quick change of channel assignments on the Oxygen8's panel, and on to the next song. I've labelled the keys 1-25 with masking tape, and then named Live's scenes correspondingly. I've assigned the knobs in various ways, depending on how I was building my Live sets at the time; 1-4 for track volumes, 5-8 for sends, and sometimes 1-8 for track volumes. The Oxygen8 has a MIDI output – you can use this to send the same info from the Oxygen8's MIDI and USB ports simultaneously. If you have 2 computers, one running Live and one running Arkaos (for example), you can trigger both at the same time, just attach a MIDI-USB

M-Audio Oxygen8

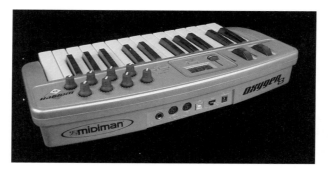

adaptor like Edirol's UM-1X to the Oxygen's MIDI out, and hook it up to your second computer. Great if you want to spread your workload over two computers. The only downer with the Oxygen8 is that, being such an 'old' product, it doesn't work with M-Audio's very useful Enigma librarian software.

Faderfox micromoduls

Faderfox's micromoduls are 'pocket sized' controllers for use with, specifically, Live and Native Instrument's Traktor (DJ software). In construction terms, they're a little more old-school than some competing products – they're tough, and they require battery or mains power (claimed 50-100 hours battery life). They also require a MIDI-USB adaptor (like Edirol's UM-1X or M-Audio's USB UNO) for connection to the computer. If you're already using a keyboard or audio interface with a MIDI input, connect a Faderfox to this with a regular MIDI cable.

(Right) M-Audio UNO

Faderfox LV-1

All Micromoduls work with Live, but the LV-1 is the most obvious match. This little box is crammed with controls: 8 faders, a crossfader, 8 assignable buttons, 4 assignable knobs, a master volume knob, a scene/track knob, and a tiny joystick. It's nice to have a MIDI controller that's small enough to carry everywhere, but useful enough to be worth carrying! Over time though, I found the LV-1's surface was too crowded... which leads neatly on to the DJ-1. It's designed for use with Traktor, but it works fine with Live. The DJ-1's interface assumes that you'll be working with 2 'decks', traditional DJ-style, labelled A and B. Each deck features knobs for Gain, High, Mid, Low, and a level fader. Other controls include knobs for filter amount and cut-off, scroll, and headphones mix, with 10 assignable buttons, a crossfader, and – again

– a shift button, for dual-function control. There are dedicated buttons for Cue A, Cue B, 1/2/3, Shift, and Select Deck. I've had fun with the DJ-1, and I prefer it to the LV-1; the layout works better with fewer controls, and it's easier to remember what everything does! Using the DJ-1 gave me some valuable ideas about how to build Live sets – DJ culture has a lot to teach musicians about performing with Live.

Faderfox DJ-1

Info – The mini-me of Live hardware setups

- 12inch Apple PowerBook G4
- Edirol FA-66 FireWire Audio/MIDI interface
- Faderfox LV-1 (sitting on top of the Edirol)

Sweet – now you can sack your roadie. For extra mini-ness, substitute a Griffin PowerMate for the Faderfox – though you'll also be sacrificing a huge amount of control if you do that.

The LV-1 and DJ-1 follow traditional layouts, but the third in the series, the LX-1, is more unusual, with 64 buttons, instead of knobs or faders (though the scene/track select knob remains). The buttons are colour coded, and labelled on the assumption that you'll be using 8 tracks in Live, providing start/stop/mute/solo/input/record/a/b for each track. But hit the group button at top left, and you'll be working with tracks 9-16. You could use the LX-1 as labelled, or use it to trigger up to 32 clips in each of 4 colour-coded tracks, or up to 16 clips in each of 8 colour-coded tracks...you get the idea.

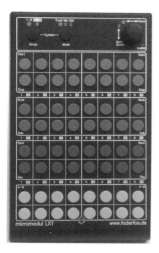

Faderfox LX-1

I get the feeling that the LX-1 should somehow be good for more experimental projects, maybe something with follow actions, or some kind of step sequencing, but I haven't really hit on it yet. I don't see the need for this number of buttons in general Live use – I'm quite happy using the keys on my computer when I want 'buttons'. The LX-1 is also hindered by the lack of overlay templates – you have to commit the assignments to memory; a good reason not to tinker with your set-up too often. At times it reminded me of M-Audio's Trigger Finger, but the Trigger Finger wins out because of its more tactile nature, and – vitally – its integration with the Enigma software editor. You can't hit either of them with drum sticks!

Faderfox suggest chaining two or three micromoduls together, to create a more comprehensive system, but these units aren't cheap. Buying two micromoduls is more expensive than a single UC33e – the UC33e provides mixer, transport, and triggering controls, and leaves the computer keyboard free for other assignments; it also features USB bus power and Enigma compatibility. The LV-1 and LX-1 do work well together: I put the LV-1 on the left of my laptop, and the LX-1 on the right. I had the LV-1 connected to the laptop, and the LX-1 chained via a regular MIDI cable. Combining units means that you can use the encoder on one for track scrolling, and the other for scene scrolling – the LEDs on both units stay in sync as you turn the encoders, so it's always clear what track you're working on. The angled design lifts the micromoduls above side-mounted FireWire and USB outputs, meaning you can get them up close to the computer instead of drifting off somewhere across the tabletop.

The Faderfoxes are over-dependent on Live's learn function – their MIDI assignments are hardwired in. Not being able to assign my preferred MIDI controllers and channels to the Faderfoxes is a serious drawback – because I use different MIDI controllers for different situations, I need to be able to swap them around without changing the MIDI assignments in my Live template every time. Although pre-configured Live templates are supplied on CD with the units, this doesn't help if you've already got a lot of Live sets mapped out, and you want to start using a micromodul.

Despite these criticisms, the micromoduls are still great little units – they can't be beaten for portability, and they're well-built. Any Live user should check them out.

Using Live without touching the computer

There's a photo on the Faderfox website of 3 micromoduls sitting astride a laptop, totally obscuring the keyboard. This implies that you can use them to run a Live set without touching your computer – there's a certain retro caveman throwback mentality that believes looking at your computer on stage is the musical version of spying on your sister taking a shower. With Live, the computer keyboard has, to a point, become a hardware controller anyway, and Live 5's expanded keyboard mapping adds to this – previously we've been restricted to using just a-z and A-Z for keyboard assignments, now we can use almost the entire keyboard.

Three Faderfoxes and a laptop

Evolution/M-Audio UC33e

The UC33e is my favourite controller for Live. With 24 knobs, 9 illuminated faders, 14 buttons, 33 presets, and Enigma support, I've spent a lot of gigs squinting at this thing. The UC33e includes a Live-specific overlay template, and this gives a good starting point for your own presets, with indications for level, pan, and effect send controls, and – on the keypad – locations for transport, tap tempo, and scene scrolling and launching. There's also 6 'spare' assignable buttons. There's a feeling of physical connection with this many controls, and it looks like you're actually doing something – maybe the audience can relate to it better, too.

The Evolution UC33e

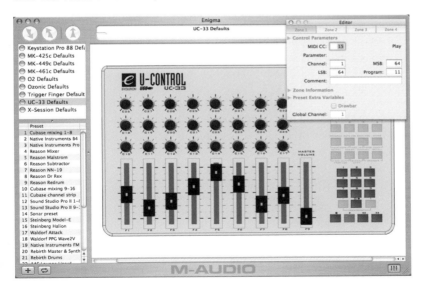

The Evolution UC33e in Enigma software

Most of my UC33e use has followed the suggested template, although I don't use Live's pan controls on stage, so I assign the 'pan' knobs to yet more effect control. I've also used it when ReWiring Live and Arkaos; using the 'pan' controls to control Arkaos' effects. I could make a separate preset for Arkaos, but I never seem to get round to it..!

Equally useful in the studio and on stage, the UC33e is still the MIDI controller to beat, and I'll be taking it on stage again very soon.

M-Audio Trigger Finger

Given M-Audio's intimate connections with Ableton (M-Audio distribute Live), Trigger Finger's suitability as a Live controller seems less than coincidental. The Trigger Finger is a USB MIDI controller for people who can't play keyboards – DJs, drummers... me. Instead of the usual 25/37/49/61/88 black and white 'proper' keyboard keys, it has 16 black rubber pads (yep, it's a lot like a USB version of Akai's ancient-but-still-popular MPC percussion sampler, the machine hip-hop was built on) – velocity and pressure sensitive – arranged in a neat grid, and four faders and eight knobs. The Trigger

The M-Audio Trigger Finger

Finger is powered via USB or an optional DC power supply, and also has a MIDI out jack. No drivers are required for Mac OSX or XP, and a free version of Live – Ableton Live Lite – is included, which although limited compared to the 'real' thing, is still a fine introduction to our favourite software (oops, we already have it!). The Trigger Finger has a threaded hole in the bottom for mic stand mounting. This is a great way to use it – the threaded hole is positioned off centre to the unit's body, centred instead on the rubber pads (which makes sense when you think about it). Don't hit it too hard!

The Trigger Finger pads/knobs

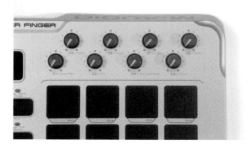

Showing laptop with Live, and Trigger Finger, on stands

Each pad is fully assignable – for different notes, channels, and velocity options; they can also send program and bank changes. There's also an assignable pressure parameter for each pad, which corresponds to aftertouch on a keyboard; possibly good for things like effects wet/dry levels. Pressure can be disabled, or you can go the other way, and send pressure only, without any notes. A note mute feature allows you to assign the pressure parameter on the pad without confusing software that's working in 'learn' mode (like Live) – otherwise the software will receive and respond to the note being sent and not the pressure. Sure you can use the Trigger Finger with Live to create percussion patterns, but Live's flexible MIDI assignment combines with the TF's programmability to do...just about anything. Because the TF is Enigma-compatible, you don't have to worry about which of your crazy set-ups to save; you can save them all! Of course Enigma makes it much easier to create those crazy set-ups in the first place, working on your computer screen instead of trying to program anything using the TF's buttons.

The Trigger Finger can store 16 presets internally. The factory default presets include two that are Live-specific – 10, which is for two Impulses on different MIDI channels, and 11, which is a general Live setup. It has to be said though, that these presets don't do anything that you couldn't achieve yourself. Preset 16 is interesting though – it's mapped to play notes from C1 to D#2, giving an unusual synth playing experience.

Info

Don't be put off if your drumming skills are even worse than mine – take advantage of Live 5's triggering and recording quantization options to ensure your hits are kept in time.

Trigger Finger in Enigma software

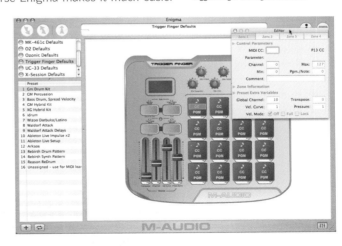

Possible Trigger Finger-oriented Live set

As above showing MIDI mapping

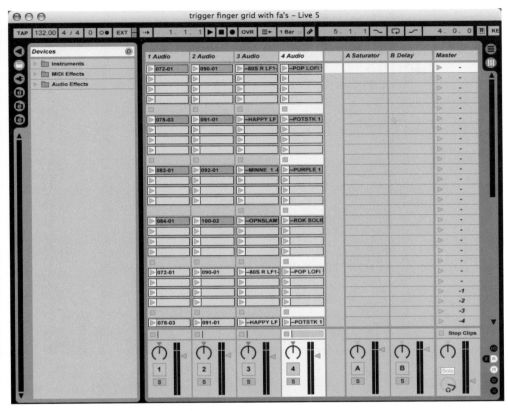

Trigger Finger set-up with follow actions

I was experimenting with a Live/Trigger Finger setup that played on the 'four of everything' setup: four tracks, with four clips in each track, then a dividing empty scene, and further groups of four. You can continue this ad infinitum using the TF's presets to send notes on different channels for each 'block'. I assigned the four faders to volume for each track, and the eight knobs went to effect sends. I used preset 5, sending on channel 5, to trigger scenes. You can see how it all works in the screen shot showing MIDI assignments; not exactly rocket science. A similar Trigger Finger setup can be used for follow actions. Use the same setup as the first one, but expand it to add follow actions below each row of triggered clips – you can add as many follow action clips as you want. It adds a random element to the pad use – see the screen shots. If you used it alongside the random MIDI system I discussed elsewhere in this book, things can get really interesting. Because the TF's pads are individually assignable, you can create little subsections on the grid; 4 pads for loops, 4 for one-shots, 4 for scenes, 4 for effects. Try assigning the pads to less likely things, maybe transport or scrolling; assign half of the pads to send MIDI to Arkaos VJ.

If you feel like a phoney, standing on stage with a keyboard, give the Trigger Finger a try. On one hand you can play logic games with it, finding correlations between Live's Session View grid, and the TF's pads, on the other you can enjoy the (relatively) physical action of (gently) striking drum pads! . And it's small enough to fit in your laptop bag. Love it.

Trigger Finger in Live with follow actions and MIDI

Info – Enigma with Live

A little while ago I helped a 'well known' dance act set up their new Live/Ozonic workstation. Thanks to Enigma, I was able to quickly create a suitable Ozonic template, and export it to disc, along with a corresponding Live set. Took it over there on a little USB flash drive – and it worked first time. Nice and easy!

Info

Before we go any further with this, be warned – the FCB manual is a stinker. What you must do – and what I did – is join the Yahoo group for FCB1010 users. Most of their posts are specific to guitar effects and amplifiers – there's little information on using Live in particular – but they know everything that you could possibly need to know about the FCB1010. There's a vast amount of information available through this group, including downloadable documents, links to software editors for PC and Mac, and firmware updates.

Behringer FCB1010 MIDI foot controller

The FCB1010 MIDI foot controller is mostly designed for guitarists who need to control MIDI-compatible effects or amplifiers. However, Live users, in their quest for strange MIDI gadgets, have discovered the FCB1010, and not just for those whose hands are kept busy playing guitar or bass or keyboards or clarinet; I've heard tell of laptop DJs using these things too.

The FCB has ten patch footswitches, up/down footswitches, and two expression pedals. A small display conveys necessary information. The footswitches correspond to ten banks, each with ten patches – so you get up to 100 patches. It's mains powered, but no wall-wart – good news. Because it's not specifically a 'computer' audio product, MIDI out is via a regular MIDI plug, so you need to get yourself a UM-1X or UNO MIDI/USB adaptor.

Any Live user could get something out of using the FCB – obviously it's relevant if your hands are busy gripping a bass or whatever, but also if you're a laptop-only performer who finds that two hands aren't enough. As usual, the only limit is your imagination. Live users have a distinct advantage with this thing, because a lot of the programming issues that drive FCB users nuts are dealt with at the Live end of things; this also helps to avoid a lot of the

FCB1010 MIDI foot controller

issues with the manual (the things that you will most likely need, like assigning MIDI notes to pedals, and copying presets, are – fortunately – described clearly enough).

The FCB1010 sends MIDI notes, CCs, and program changes, so all of the usual Live functions can be controlled. Use the footswitches for transport, scrolling, scene selection, effects, etc. One thing to remember is that MIDI notes are actually sent with a preset; you must send a preset to send a note! Once you remember that, it's quite simple. The expression pedals are fun – you can assign them to volume, pan, filters, effect wet/dry mixes – even song tempo, which is quite perverse because it's very difficult to control in fine increments! You can specify the notes sent by the switches, so you can even use it to play notes in Operator, for that 1970s Moog Taurus vibe. If you try my MIDI setup clip idea (see Chapter 7 'Live Talks To Itself'), you can use the FCB to summon a whole new mixer setup in-between or during songs. The FCB1010 can use different channel numbers for different commands, ie

Ripwerx FCB software editor

channel 1 for MIDI notes, and channel 2 MIDI CCs, but unfortunately the banks and patches can't store different channel numbers – it would be nice to be able to send channel 1 from bank 1, channel 2 from bank 2, etc; apparently MIDI routing utilities such as ControlAid and MIDI Ox can add a lot of extra functionality to the FCB1010.

Even in the studio, working with a foot controller puts a different perspective on things – I like to work standing up anyway, so it's a natural extension of that. These pedal-based set-ups eat floor space, though – the FCB1010, a laptop stand, and if you add guitar or bass pedals like the GT-6B – that's a lot of tap dancing.

The FCB1010 is an ideal control choice for Live-using instrumentalists and vocalists. For non-instrumentalists who want something other than a keyboard to work with, it's an unusual option, but one that keeps your hands free so you can do even more.

Jesse Terry uses the FCB1010 on stage:

Info

A common problem with the FCB seems to be that the expression pedals don't appear to work when you first get the unit. There's a calibration procedure which should solve the problem – it worked for me. Rather than reproduce that info here, I suggest that you get the latest info via the FCB users' forum; that'll guarantee it's as up to date as possible.

Quote – Jesse Terry

I use a guitar with a MIDI pickup, going into ControlAid, then Live & Reason. I use one expression pedal to scroll between tracks (3 keyboards, 2 guitar, 1 bass and 1 with program change MIDI clips going to my Line 6 Pod XT box), and Control Aid routes the 10 buttons on my FCB 1010 to whichever track I am in." (Jesse also told me about something he used in a previous band; Circular Logic's InTime – software which enables applications such as Live to sync to real-time input from a drummer or percussionist – like an ongoing tap tempo function. This is a role reversal if ever there was one – instead of following a click in his headphones, the drummer is telling the computer what to do! This has great potential if you want to use Live in a band situation – of course you'll some sort of MIDI pads or MIDI triggers for acoustic drums.

Mackie Control Universal

Live 5 includes out-of-the-box support for the Mackie Control Universal, which offers a unique advantage over using Live with regular MIDI hardware controls – the MCU and Live can enjoy a caring, sharing, two way relationship; any changes made on one are immediately reflected in the other. The Control is just that though – a controller; you still need an audio interface. It's also not particularly portable – more of a studio than performance item. MCU-compatibility has become a standard, though, and there are other devices which take advantage of the MCU's communication skills, while adding that audio functionality – including the Yamaha O1x, and, recently, the M-Audio ProjectMix IO. These 'newcomers' use FireWire to connect to computers, and include audio interfaces, becoming true 'all-in-one' solutions (and the ProjectMix features Pro Tools MP compatibility). Any of these units will help you keep your eyes and hands off the computer – if that matters to you. Last minute update: the ProjectMix, after an initial period of being sold 'alone', will only be available as a bundle with Ableton Live!

M-Audio Ozonic

Think Oxygen8 meets FW410 meets UC33 in a dark alley – a FireWire alley. The Ozonic combines elements from each of these devices; 37-note keyboard, faders, knobs, and buttons, joystick, and transport controls, all connected to your computer with one FireWire cable. The top panel hosts an array of level-related controls, allowing the mixing of the Ozonic's two out-

M-Audio Ozonic top view

M-Audio Ozonic rear view

put pairs, and monitoring controls for input sources; DJ cueing/pre listening can be set up just as easily as monitoring for recording.

Round back is a single FireWire port, MIDI in/out ports, sustain/expression pedal outputs, 4 analog jack outputs, a headphone output, and 4 analog jack inputs – one is a mic input with phantom power.

The Ozonic takes the 'use Live without looking at the screen concept' quite a long way. Your computer screen can take a little bit of a back seat when you use this thing. If you really work with it, it does start to feel like you're using a keyboard workstation. The Ozonic is well laid out – a lot of controls, but they don't feel crowded, and everything is in a logical place. As usual with M-Audio gear, all buttons, knobs, and faders are individually assignable to different MIDI channels, and this is made easier by Enigma compatibility (there are also 20 onboard preset slots).

M-Audio Ozonic in Enigma

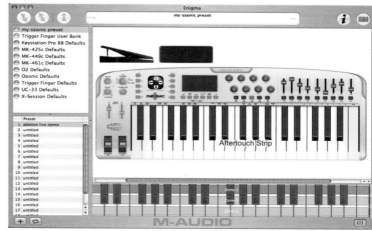

For use with Live, I set up the Ozonic like this (see screenshot and photo):

Rewind button = scroll scenes up
Stop button = stop transport
Record button = fire scene
Play button = start transport
Fast forward button = scroll scenes down
Knobs 1-8 = pan tracks 1-8
Faders 1-8 = level tracks 1-8
Fader 9 = master track level
Buttons under faders = solo tracks 1-8
Button under fader 9 = stop all clips
Keys numbered 1-37 for triggering scenes, loops, and one-shots.

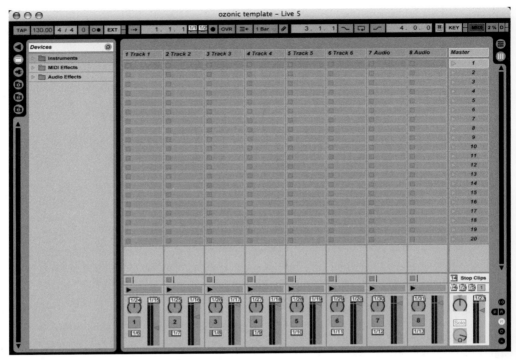

Live controller map for Ozonic

Any all-in-one unit makes certain compromises; the Ozonic has fewer inputs and outputs than the FW410 or FA-66. For maximum ins/outs use a dedicated FireWire audio interface, with a separate keyboard/controller hooked up via USB. Other than that, though, it's pretty complete, and relatively portable. You probably won't be taking it to your local Coffee Republic, but it's very neatly-sized for gig use, or for taking to your friend's place for a jam. As far as FireWire all-in-ones with built-in keyboards are concerned, this is it.

Overlay template for Live

DIY template

I've already mentioned how Live 5 brings expanded keyboard mapping. I've been trying to come up with a more-or-less standard set-up, that I can use for all of my live (small 'l') sets. Raidius make the FinalKeys – flexible plastic overlays for computer keyboards, and I've used one of these as the basis for my Live overlay. See the photo for my working layout; I've done a couple of

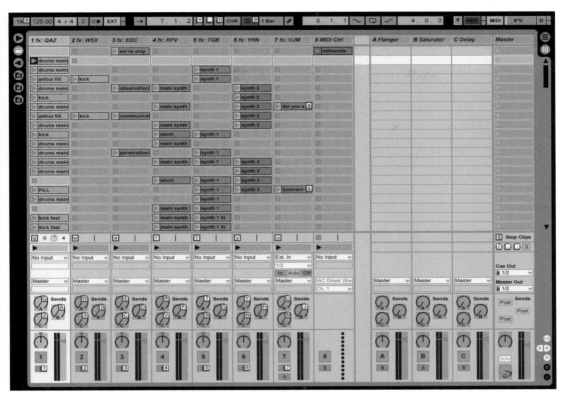

Live keyboard map for overlay template

gigs using this template, and if you're in the mood to leave your hardware at home, this might help. The only problem with an entirely 'qwerty' based system is that you can't do any incremental changes, like with knobs or faders – everything is either very ON or very OFF, so if you use 'z' to activate a delay, you're going to get the whole thing all at once when you hit 'z'. I put the wet/dry mix of my send effects at a fairly low level, and then use key mapping to bump the send knob for that effect full on. It gives me a fast effect on/off, at a workable level, and I can always use the trackpad to make finer adjustments up or down if I need to.

Jazz Mutant Lemur

Jazz Mutant's Lemur is a 12inch touch screen control interface for music software. Originally based on OSC (Open Sound Control), regular MIDI functionality has just arrived, and there are already Live templates available on the website. The Lemur allows you to design your own interface, based on a library of buttons, faders, etc, and connects to your computer via the ethernet port. The addition of MIDI, and therefore Live compatibility, is a last-minute development at the time of writing; I suggest you keep an eye on this product – the only thing that could stop Lemur's progress is the high price.

The Lemur controller

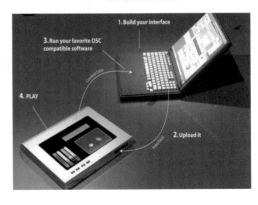

PowerMate

Not actually MIDI: the Griffin Technology PowerMate

The PowerMate is basically a giant aluminium knob that plugs into your computer via USB. It performs up to six actions, and each can be assigned to a key on your computer keyboard, or a combination of key actions. The actions are turn left, turn right, click-turn left, click-turn right, click, and long click. The PowerMate control panel allows you to save command combinations for different applications, so as well as using it as a general purpose media player control, for example, you can use it as a bare-bones Live controller. Use it to scroll through and trigger scenes or clips, as a master volume, click to select a fader, then turn the knob, transport control, jog-shuttle – anything that an action on the computer keyboard can do. as I said, it also stores key combinations, so you can use it to show/hide Live interface elements such as the mixer. It'll work alongside other USB devices, so it might make a handy companion to a USB MIDI controller. No, you can't use two PowerMates simultaneously – a shame. PowerMate is also a fine piece of USB eye candy, it has a pulsing blue light in its base, which looks coooool.

The PowerMate control panel

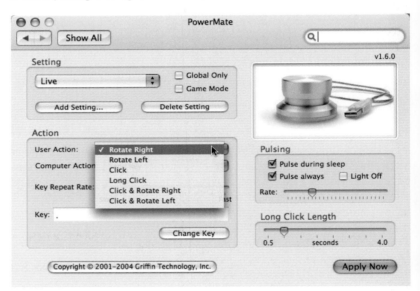

Some people use the PowerMate for a basic DJing setup – if you work with a song per clip, you can use it to scroll through songs, and then trigger them.

Live's pseudo-MIDI keyboard

There's no way to get Live's 'virtual' typing-to-MIDI keyboard to act as a remote control, it only works for sending notes to software instruments. Remember that if any function/note assignments have already been made, those notes won't be triggered by the computer keyboard. Also remember to refer to the Status Bar at the bottom of the Live screen when you're assigning MIDI parameters or using the pseudo-keyboard.

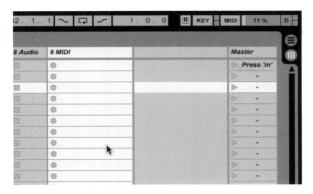

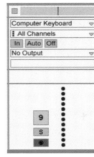

(Left) Computer keyboard input button

(Right) Input arming for computer keyboard

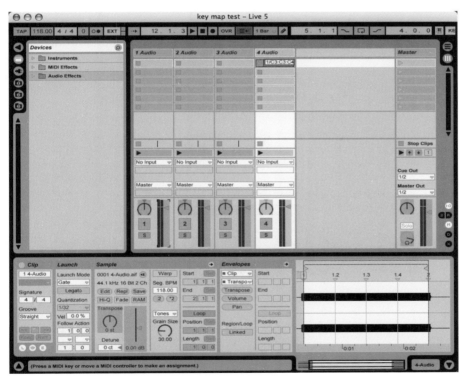

Quick MIDI keyboard mapping

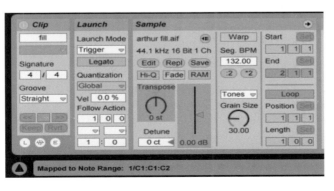

Close up of status bar at bottom of Live screen

Quick MIDI keyboard mapping

You need a controller keyboard plugged in for this to work. When you have a clip mapped to a MIDI note, hit Ctrl-m/cmd-m, and when you click on the clip, you'll get a Status Bar message saying: 'Mapped to Channel/Note: 1/C0 (or whatever) (Press multiple keys above or below this one to define a note range.)' Hold down, say C-2 and C2, and then hit Ctrl-m/cmd-m to exit midi mapping mode. Now play your keyboard within the defined range, and you'll hear that clip pitched up and down across the keys. This is a fast way of getting a sample working for you, and it saves filling your screen with multiple, differently-pitched, copies of the same clip.

You could use it to create a cruder version of an existing sound in your synth or sampler. Create an audio recording of a single C note, say 'C0'. Then assign low and high MIDI notes to it as described above, so that the sound is 'forced' to play over a range of a couple of octaves. This will undo a lot of careful work somebody has done to make something sound and behave like a 'proper' sample – so what?

This feature may seem redundant, when it's so easy to just drop a sample into Simpler, and achieve better results, but it's quick and dirty, and that's good!

Using Live 5 with audio and MIDI interfaces

If your computer has a good quality stereo audio output, there'll be a lot of times when that's enough – if you're using headphones, or hooked up to your hi-fi speakers; even playing live sometimes. Eventually though, you'll be irresistibly drawn to audio interfaces – boxes which connect to your computer, usually via FireWire or USB (USB1 or USB2, but 2 is preferable), and provide better quality inputs/outputs (and more of them), allowing you to route many tracks of audio in and out simultaneously. These interfaces range in size from small, portable units to rack mounted studio models. The smaller ones are typically bus-powered, taking their juice directly from the computer via a USB or FireWire cable. Many audio interfaces also include MIDI inputs/outputs; another dimension is added when you include MIDI controller hardware – with piano-style keys, and/or knobs, or faders, or joysticks – that also has built-in audio and MIDI interface features; see the Yamaha 01x and M-Audio Ozonic for examples of this philosophy.

Edirol FA-66 FireWire compact audio/MIDI interface

The FA-66 is a very small (and therefore portable) FireWire audio/MIDI interface with a tough red metal case; it's Mac OSX and Windows XP compatible. It can be FireWire bus-powered, and includes a built-in limiter. The front panel features two XLR/TRS combo inputs with phantom power and input sensitivity knobs, a Hi-Z (high impedance) button for the second input, a digital input select switch, direct monitoring knob and soft ctrl switch (for direct monitor control via ASIO software), stereo/mono select, phones socket, and master volume knob. The rear panel's got DC mains power in (for computers that don't provide enough bus power), power switch, 4- and 6-pin FireWire ports, sample rate select switch (from 44.1-192 kHz), phantom power switch, limiter switch, 4 1/4" phono outputs, MIDI in, MIDI out, S/PDIF digital in and out, phonos for inputs 3 and 4, and an input level knob for 3 & 4. The built-in limiter is a good idea – preventing distortion on incoming signals without having to use a separate hardware (or software) limiter.

FA-66 front and rear

The FA-66 doesn't need the computer to be shut down every time it's attached/detached to/from the computer; something which is required for M-Audio FireWire devices; if you're constantly packing/unpacking your gear (which I am), this quickly becomes annoying. The FA-66 doesn't have the most outputs – a maximum of 6 are available, depending on sample rates – but for musicians in small studios or doing small gigs, it's enough (DJs note – Live allows you to send Cue outputs to the FA-66's 3/4 outputs, but you'll need to add a mixer for headphone monitoring, unless you're a Mac user – see below). Good news for Mac users is that it's fully compatible with OSX's FireWire and MIDI drivers – no driver installation is required; at a recent gig I was able to lend the FA-66 to another PowerBook user, who needed it at the last minute. It's an exercise in minimalism – small case, slim manual, no drivers (for Mac users) – and no software mixer for routing flexibility; this is something included with M-Audio's interfaces, but not everybody will miss it.

Use the Direct Monitor knob when you're recording an instrument into a Live set that already has some tracks with audio. The knob balances audio from the computer with any incoming signal. If you deactivate the receiving live track, it'll still record from the FA-66, but won't output any audio at all, that guarantees you're just hearing the FA-66 input. These can be useful features if you're dealing with latency problems, especially combined with Live 5's Device delay compensation, and Track Delay.

My FA-66 set-up: FireWire to/from PowerBook/Live 5; MIDI cable out to Boss GT-6B bass effects processor, stereo phonos out to amp and speakers, front XLRs in L&R from GT-6B.

The FA-66 is a great box – it's been reliable in both studio and performance environments; no unexpected pops or clicks, and Live has never failed to recognise it. It's quite resilient – although it's not something that's recommended, there's been a couple of times when I've forgotten to connect the FA-66 before launching Live, and I've plugged it in regardless, and Live has recognised it without problems. This kind of reliability definitely takes the pressure off in live situations!

M-Audio FW410 FireWire audio/MIDI interface

Slightly heftier than the FA-66, is the M-Audio FW410 – another mobile FireWire audio/MIDI interface. There are many similarities between the two, but the FW410 is distinguished by a greater number of inputs/outputs, and a second headphone socket, with a dedicated volume knob (excellent). Unfortunately the FW410 needs the computer to be shut down before connection/disconnection (not unusual with FireWire peripherals, to be fair).

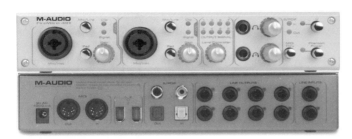

Front and rear of the FW410

Unlike the FA-66, drivers are required for OSX and XP – installation also places a software control panel, with a mixer page, on your computer, giving the FW410 extra routing flexibility; for example it's possible to create a separate headphone mix, so that if you're working with a musician who wants to hear things a certain way, maybe with some reverb on a voice, you can give them that without committing to the effect. The software mixer also allows direct monitoring to be setup with the FW410, so if you're experiencing insurmountable latency problems when recording, you can mix your incoming audio signal with your backing track – so you're hearing the incoming audio as it arrives at the FW410, rather than after it's been through your computer. It's also possible to create an aux feed so you can add effects to the direct signal, without committing them to disk. If you want something that's still small enough to be portable, and you need 10 outputs and advanced routing options, try the FW410. It's also good for surround!

Info

Choosing the right audio interface depends on what exactly you plan to do with it. The biggest problem is software drivers; if your system's working perfectly, avoid jumping on the latest driver update; let somebody else be the guinea pig! I've experienced some really frustrating problems relating to driver updates for audio interfaces – that's why, as a Mac user, I welcome the driver-free FA-66.

Set up a laptop jam with an FW410

Add two sets of headphones, and one mini jack to L/R phono/jack 'y' lead. Laptop A has the FW410 running with Live. Laptop B sends its output via the headphone socket, through the Y lead, to the FW410' s 1/2 inputs. Laptop A then takes the input from the Laptop B to, say, track 5, and record/monitors it, so they can hear it in their headphones (which are connected to the FW410, not the laptop). Laptop B's owner can then plug into the second headphone socket and hear it too. Instant laptop jam, using the FW410 as a bus-powered interface and headphone mixer (with a separate volume control for each)! Whoever's using Laptop A can sample, and apply effects to, Laptop B's output. Cool.

Combo audio/MIDI interfaces/controllers

FireWire audio/MIDI interfaces are now readily available; rarer are the true do-it-all devices that combine audio/MIDI interface and hardware MIDI controller. For examples of these see the Yamaha 01x, M-Audio Ozonic, and the new M-Audio ProjectMix I/O. If you're building a system totally from scratch, one of these will cover all your needs in a single box, with just one cable required...jump to 'Using Live 5 With Hardware Controllers' to read more about these!

The Yamaha 01x

ProjectMix I/O

Live and multiple audio interfaces

I'm showing my Mac bias again here. Live will only identify one audio interface at a time. However, OSX 10.4 (aka Tiger) recognises multiple audio interfaces, and combines them to create an 'aggregate' device with extra outputs – you can create various configurations and name/save them. Better still, the Mac's built-in audio system can be included as a device. Launch Live, and the aggregate appears just like a regular audio interface. This is a way of using the FA-66 to prelisten for DJing, even though it doesn't appear to support that in hardware. Send your master tracks out to the PA via the FA-66, and the cue output via the Mac's built-in audio, where you can listen to it on headphones.

Mac OSX aggregate devices panel

Aggregate device selection in Live preferences

Specific aggregate outputs in Live's Session view

Get more sounds

Everybody wants more sounds, no matter what instrument they play. In electronic music the search is never-ending – a 'new sound' can be an effect, or a sample, or a new software instrument. Here's some ways Live users can add new sounds to their collection…

Samples on disc

Sample discs range from modest audio CDs to host-specific DVD-ROM packages such as the Reason Drum Kits collection. No matter how hardcore you are about creating your own sounds, there are times when boil-in-the-bag samples, especially drum loops, are a real lifesaver. Composers working in commercial environments are especially grateful for this kind of themed sample collection – they make it easy to get an 'appropriate' groove going quickly. If you built an entire song just using untreated loops from sample CDs, it would be pretty sterile-sounding, but Live excels at sonic manipulation – the more you mangle, the better it gets! At the simplest level there are sample sets on audio CD, guaranteeing universal compatibility at low cost (there's a lot less preparation time involved for the manufacturer).

Club Spectrum sample disc cover

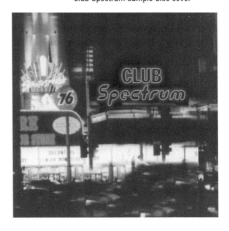

Info – iTunes is your friend

You'll need to manage the many audio samples that you'll collect. iTunes is the free music/video player/librarian from Apple, available for Mac OSX and Windows XP – you probably have it on your computer already. iTunes' folders and playlists are just as good for organising loops and one-shots as they are entire songs. Direct one of Live's three File Browsers to your iTunes Music folder, or a sub-folder within that; if you're into DJing with Live, you can keep your pre-warped songs in an iTunes playlist, so you can easily access them from either application. Import your samples into iTunes making sure 'Copy files to iTunes Music folder when adding to library' is selected in iTunes Preferences/Advanced.

Live can grab tracks straight from audio CDs, and they'll be auto warped like any other material (make sure you save your set as self-contained afterwards, otherwise you'll be in trouble when you eject the CD).

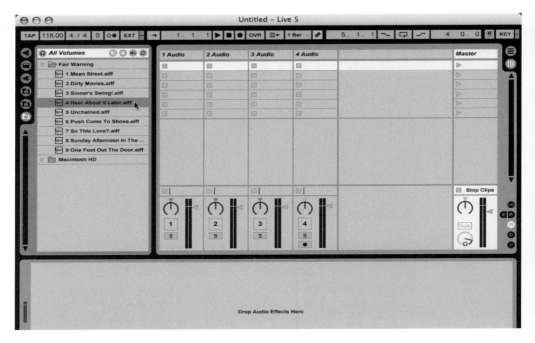

Songs on CD being previewed

A song loading and auto warping from
CD

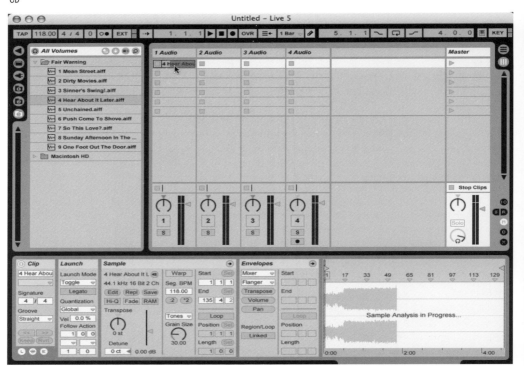

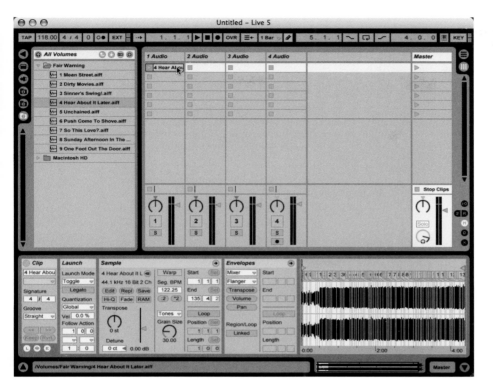

Showing a fully auto warped song from CD

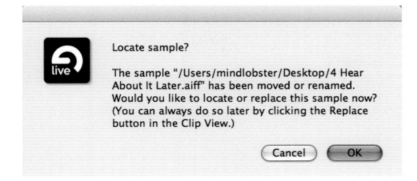

The error message if CD song isn't included in self-contained set

If you're online when you insert a mass-produced audio CD in your computer and you have iTunes open, it'll get the song titles for you, and Live's Browser will update to display the same info. Drag your chosen song/s from the Browser straight into the Session or Arrangement View, then use Live's Save Set Self-Contained option to include a copy of the song/s when you save the Live set.

More expensive than audio CDs are format-specific discs (which can be CD or DVD). Where audio CDs contain straightforward loops and sounds, these discs contain ready-to-go software instrument banks and patches, as well as folders containing basic audio files. Live doesn't support any major

The Kontakt interface

sample formats as such – it has its own samplers in Impulse and Simpler – but of course it'll host your AU or VST sampler, and there are expansion discs available for all sampler formats – Reason (NNXT and Rex2), EXS, HALion, Kontakt, etc. A recent development is sample packages with their own sampler interface, usually based on Native Instrument's Kontakt, so you don't need to already be a user of a particular sampling platform.

Online samples

Online libraries allow you to pick and choose individual samples, instead of buying entire discs; a good option if you just want to grab a quick sound effect or beat. Powerfx are 'old-timers' in this field now, and their site currently offers material in various styles including ambient, blues, classical, electronica, and hip hop, and in formats such as Acid, NNXT, EXS, HALion, Rex2, and Apple Loops. You should also check out The Freesound Project, which is (in their words) "a collaborative database of Creative Commons licensed sounds". The sounds available are quite diverse, but mostly focussed on electronic, field recordings, and experimental sources.

Apple Loops

Owners of GarageBand-equipped Macs will find their computers contain a number of Apple Loops (basically fancy AIFs, for Live's purposes), which can be drag'n'dropped straight into a Live set, and treated exactly like regular AIFs. If you install anything like Logic or Soundtrack Pro, you'll end up with thousands of these things.

Reason Refills

You already know how Reason and Live can snuggle up close to each other, and how Live can share Reason's sounds via ReWire. As well as commercial-ly-available Reason Refills from people like Time+Space, there are many free or cheap – and good – Refills available on the web; the only things I use Reason for these days. See Kreativ Sounds (their Analog BASStard is great), and Reason Banks (their Analog Monsters collections are must-haves for all Reason users).

Using Live 5 with Stylus RMX

Spectrasonics' Stylus RMX is a good example of a third-party instrument plug-in; a drum module which runs as an AU, VST or RTAS. It installs a 7.4 GB sound library, and has a mixer page, and built-in effects, including com-pression, distortion, and delay. Up to eight patterns can play simultaneous-ly, whether full drum loops or individual percussion parts. Each of these 8 parts can be assigned to a separate stereo output – so, each can be routed to a separate Live track for mixing/processing. Although at times Stylus RMX is a bit of a monster (too much interface, if you see what I mean), it contains great material, in a more-or-less accessible format. Spectrasonics should be complimented on their support for RMX – there are *hours* of tutorial QuickTime movies, including specific information on using it with Live.

The Stylus RMX mixer page

The Stylus RMX effects page

Assigning Stylus outputs to Live inputs

By default, RMX sends all eight tracks to a master stereo output. However, it's easy to change this so that some or all of the tracks go to individual tracks in Live. Go to the Stylus mixer page, and load a drum part in each of the eight tracks. Then click on the 'OUT A' box at the left of each track. It'll pop up a list from OUT A to OUT H. Assign each Stylus track to a different letter: A-H.

Stylus RMX output selection

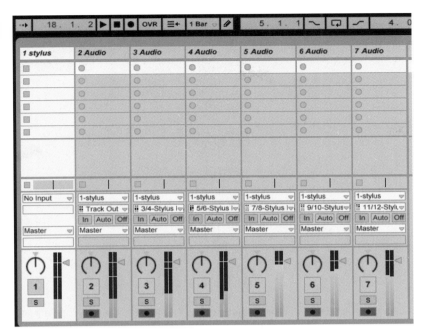

Return to your Live window, and create eight new audio tracks. For each one, select a Stylus output from A-H as the input source, then arm the track. Now you can apply Live's effects to individual Stylus parts, and of course record each part into a new clip within Live. Remember that you can also do this kind of routing exercise with Impulse!

If you're into beat driven music, you could do an entire slammin live set with just Live, RMX, and no other instruments or sources – triggering the beats and editing effects with a hardware controller like the Trigger Finger. It's also possible to edit RMX parts by dragging the selected part into a Live MIDI track and treating it like any other clip. Of course, Stylus beats are

included in your stereo renders, just like with any other plug-in. You can't crack open RMX's audio content, but if there's a particular hit that you want to grab, trigger it from a controller, or Live's pseudo-MIDI keyboard, and record it into an audio clip, then drop it into Impulse to build an 'RMX' kit.

Live's own drum sampler, Impulse, is great – you don't need anything else, but if you insist on more drums, Stylus is a good way to go.

Trackteam Audio Livefills

Trackteam were the first to release CDs containing Live content (presets for instruments and effects, MIDI and audio clips) that install directly into the Live 5 Library. They've even created lesson files that are accessed in the same way as Live's lessons, right in the Live interface itself. Hopefully the range will expand to include more Operator presets and Live Clips; at the moment there are three sets available: Tacklebox, Beatbox, and Travelbox. These sets are cutely-packaged (important), very affordable, and highly recommended.

Ableton Live Packs

Ableton are now releasing their own Live Packs – collections of presets and Live Clips. These packs take advantage of the new Live Clip format introduced with Live 5, and install directly into the library, for immediate browsing. Hopefully Live Packs will allow Ableton to provide us with some provocative material, instead of the homogenous gloop that usually marks the widespread acceptance of a music application – how many Apple Loops do you need?

Add-ons like these, from both Trackteam and Ableton themselves, will help us access more and better sounds, without having to ReWire to other applications – keeping everything within the familiar and functional Live interface.

Operator

Operator was controversial on its initial release – its inclusion in demo form within Live 4.1 aggravated people who thought it should be cheaper (or free), and some objected to the fact that it was Live-specific, and couldn't be used within other sequencers. Operator has gone on to be appreciated as a powerful creative tool that has the advantage of seamless integration with the Live environment. Some of Operator's sounds are quite underwhelming when heard in isolation, but they work great in mixes – which is what matters. Operator is a great source of new sounds, and it's right under our noses; we just have to figure out how it works! Before you spend money on CDs or sam-

Operator

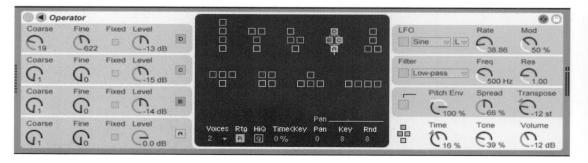

plers, take the time to study Operator, Impulse, and Simpler; they shouldn't be underrated.

Info – Live resource management

I don't use any software samplers or instruments on stage; I render everything as audio clips in advance – it's a lot more flexible for live use, because then I can move clips between tracks more easily; it's also less demanding of my laptop.

Record your own

Live is a sampler. Record audio straight into it; mix and match sources – microphone/pre amp, your computer's built-in mic, minidisc, your phone...Live rules in these collage-type situations. I love MacMice's MicFlex USB microphone, a mono USB mic on a flexible metal arm (I mentioned it earlier in 'Performance Notes'). It slots into a desktop base, for that radio announcer vibe, or the flexible portion can plug directly into a free USB port; probably the most minimal way to add a microphone to your Live setup.

External sound generators

Live can send MIDI to control external synths or samplers. If you've got some old gear getting dusty in the corner – use it or sell it! For Live, this is effectively the same as communicating with other software – see preferences for MIDI/Sync settings, and remember you can send bank and program changes from MIDI clips.

External DSP cards

How about working with an external box like TC Electronics' FireWire Compact – the modern version of the hardware sound module? This one connects via FireWire, and integrates right into your computer setup, with each

effect or instrument appearing as a plug-in. The Compact features useful studio effects such as compression and reverb, but also includes a synth based on the Roland SH101. The Compact is expandable, adding synths like the Access Virus and Novation V-Station. The Compact has no physical audio connections, just FireWire – the audio signal routes out of Live exactly as with any other plug-in. Tragically for laptop geeks like me, the Compact is not bus-powered!

Appendix

Links

Ableton www.ableton.com
You guessed it – makers of Ableton Live 5. The forum is worth regular visits.

Apple www.apple.com
Desktop and laptop computers, GarageBand, Logic, Soundtrack Pro, iPod, iTunes; information on recording, podcasting, etc.

Audacity: http://audacity.sourceforge.net
Free audio editor for Mac OSX, Windows, and Linux.

Behringer www.behringer.com
Makers of FCB1010 MIDI foot controller, and various other MIDI control devices.

Behringer FCB1010 Yahoo Users Group http://groups.yahoo.com/group/fcb1010
Support group for users of the FCB1010; this group makes all the difference between success and failure with your FCB.

Boss www.roland.com
Makers of GT-6B bass effects processor.

Circular Logic www.circular-logic.com
Makers of the InTime tempo sync system.

ControlAid www.charlie-roberts.com/controlAid
Incredibly useful MIDI routing utility for Mac OSX.

Cubase www.steinberg.net
Leading cross-platform 'traditional' DAW – digital audio workstation.

Echo Audio www.echoaudio.com
The Indigo DJ audio output card for laptops.

Edirol www.edirol.co.uk, www.edirol.com
Various USB and FireWire interfaces and controllers.

Ergo Phizmiz www.ergophizmiz.com
Prolific Live user who loves to jam in the Arrangement View.

Faderfox www.faderfox.de
Extremely portable Live-specific MIDI controllers.

John 00 Fleming www.john00fleming.com
DJ...writer...Live user!

Freesound http://freesound.iua.upf.edu
Archive of sounds available under Creative Commons license.

GarageBand www.apple.com/garageband
Apple's low cost DAW, ReWire friendly.

Granted Software www.grantedsw.com
ReVision, the ReWire movie player.

Griffin Technology www.griffintechnology.com
PowerMate USB knob controller.

Glideascope www.glideascope.com
Live-using downtempo trip hop artist.

Hubi's MIDI Loopback http://members.nextra.at/hubwin/midi.html
Popular MIDI routing utility

InStand www.instand.com
Innovative laptop stands suitable for performance use.

Jazz Mutant www.jazzmutant.com
The radical Lemur touch screen control surface.

J-Lab www.jlabmusic.com
Ableton Live-steeped laptop performer.

Junxion www.steim.org
Send MIDI with game controllers.

Keith Lang www.songcarver.com
Live-using performer and software developer. See also: www.cocoajackson-lane.com, for info on Keith's band.

Logic www.apple.com
Apple's powerful DAW, in Express and Pro versions.

Mackie www.mackie.com
They do the Mackie Control Universal, a hardware control surface supported by Live 5.

M-Audio www.maudio.co.uk, www.m-audio.com
An enormous range of USB and FireWire audio/MIDI interfaces, controllers, etc. UK/US distributors of Ableton Live.

MDA www.mda-vst.com
Some of the best free AU and VST plug-ins around.

MidiO http://home.comcast.net/~retroware RetroWare
AU plug-in which allows GarageBand to send MIDI to applications such as Live.

MIDI Ox www.midiox.com
Self-proclaimed 'world's greatest all-purpose MIDI utility'.

MIDI Yoke www.midiox.com
MIDI patching utility.

mindlobster www.mindlobster.com
Live-obsessed laptop performer and producer with highly visual live show.

MOTU www.motu.com
MOTU 828 FireWire audio interface, amongst other things.

Musolomo www.plasq.com
Innovative plug-in sampler instrument.

Native Instruments www.nativeinstruments.com
Software: Absynth, B4, FM7, Kontakt, Pro53, Reaktor.

Novation www.novationmusic.com
The Remote25 MIDI controller.

Nusystems www.nusystems.co.uk
Pre-installed music computer systems, laptop and desktop varieties.

OSC www.opensoundcontrol.com
Multi media control protocol, designed to 'replace' MIDI.

PC Publishing www.pc-publishing.com
They published this book!

Pluggo www.cycling74.com
Plug-in suite, but not like all the rest!

PowerFX www.powerfx.com
Online and on-disc resource for audio samples in various formats.

Pro Tools www.digidesign.com
The pro's DAW.

Public Loop www.publicloop.com
Pioneering educational project based around Ableton Live and Arkaos VJ.

RadiaL www.cycling74.com
Loop-based performance software from the Pluggo people.

Raidius www.raidius.com
FinalKeys computer keyboard overlays – make your own Live controller template.

Reason www.propellerheads.se
Reason self-contained software studio, an excellent sound source for Live.

ReVision www.grantedsw.com
ReWire master QuickTime movie player.

Saytek www.saytek.co.uk
Live-using performer.

Sound On Sound www.soundonsound.com
Hype-free music technology magazine.

Spectrasonics www.spectrasonics.com
Stylus RMX, AU/VST drum unit.

Tacklebox www.trackteamaudio.com
Add-on packs of presets and samples for LIve's instruments.

Jesse Terry http://music.download.com/jethro
Live/FCB1010-using artist.

Time+Space www.timespace.com
Major providers of virtual instruments, sample CDs, etc.

Jody Wisternoff www.wayoutwest.uk.com
Jody's from Way Out West, the Bristol-based DJs/remixers/producers.

Yamaha www.yamahasynth.com
01x audio-MIDI interface/controller/mixer, compatible with Live 5 via Mackie Control support.

Joe Young www.theplaysthething.com
Live-using composer, working in theatre and dance.

Hans Zimmer www.hans-zimmer.com
Live-savvy Hollywood soundtrack whiz.

Top ten keyboard shortcuts

Some of these are keyboard shortcuts that I use a lot – and some are ones I should use a lot...(showing Windows/Mac versions).

1 Tab – toggle Arrangement and Session.

2 F11/Ctrl F11 – enter/exit full screen.

3 Shift-F12 – show/hide Track/Clip View.

4 Ctrl l/Cmd l = create loop from selection. also activates loop button if not already on.

5 Right-click/Ctrl-click – show context menu.

6 Ctrl k/Cmd k – Key Map Mode.

7 Ctrl m/Cmd m – MIDI Map Mode.

8 Ctrl-shift-k/Cmd-shift-k – Computer MIDI Keyboard on/off.

9 Ctrl j/Cmd j – Consolidate.

10 F1 – F8 = activate/deactivate tracks 1– 8

Index